FOCUSED MINDS!

GAURANGA DARSHAN DAS

ILLUSTRATIONS
CHARBAK DIPTA

SCHOLASTIC
New York Toronto London Auckland
Sydney New Delhi Hong Kong

Published by Scholastic India Pvt. Ltd.
A subsidiary of Scholastic Inc., New York, 10012 (USA).
Publishers since 1920, with international operations in Canada, Australia, New Zealand, the United Kingdom, India, and Hong Kong.

For information regarding permission, write to:
Scholastic India Pvt. Ltd.
A-27, Ground Floor, Sigma Centre
Infocity-1, Sector 34, Gurgaon-122001 (India)

First edition: April 2025

ISBN-13: 978-93-5954-679-7

Printed in India at Sai Printo Pack Pvt. Ltd.

Every child has a spark of untapped focus,
an effulgent journey waiting to ignite.
Empower them with insights from the Bhagavad Gita,
and watch them shine with clarity and purpose.

Author's Note

In today's world of endless choices, even sticking to our favourite *distractions* has become a challenge. From delighting in games set in the metaverse to ordering fast food at the press of a button, convenience seems to be the ultimate pursuit even if such activities slow us down and adversely affect our health.

But what if I told you that cultivating a focused mind could be just as easy and enjoyable as savouring your favourite fruit cake? Rooted in the timeless wisdom of the Bhagavad Gita, *Focused Minds!* invites you to explore lesser-known yet powerful ways of developing unwavering focus. This journey unfolds across two engaging sections.

The first section introduces you to the deeper workings of your mind and the mysteries of the visible and invisible aspects of yourself. Discover the interconnections between your mind and intelligence, and explore the dynamics of a healthy ego versus an unhealthy one.

The second section takes you on a journey from distraction to concentration, offering practical techniques and revealing several secrets to attaining true focus.

These profound concepts are brought to life through engaging conversations, lively illustrations, and thought-provoking discussions that make the learning process vibrant and far from ordinary.

As you embark on the rewarding process of nurturing a focused mind, may the distractions you leave behind find their rightful place elsewhere. Though this book is designed for kids, its lessons offer immense value to anyone seeking to improve their mental, emotional, and physical well-being.

So, let's begin this exciting adventure together—where we'll learn to be less distracted, focus more, and embrace the joy of clarity and purpose!

– Gauranga Darshan Das

Contents

SECTION 1: KNOW YOUR MIND 1

Chapter 1: **The Body-dress** 2
Who Am I?
The Gita's First Lesson

Chapter 2: **The Tale of Two Bodies** 8
The Mystery of the Invisible Body
The Wonders of the Subtle Body

Chapter 3: **The Mind's Desires and Emotions** 14
Anu's Desires Fulfilled!
How Do Desires and Emotions Enter Your Mind?
How Does the Mind Influence the Body?

Chapter 4: **Intelligence: The Mind's Friend** 20
Control the Kite of Your Mind
Hierarchy of Elements in Our Bodies
The Body Chariot
The First Mindfulness Tip

Chapter5: **Ego: The Mind's Boss** 26
Two Friends Who Became Enemies
False Ego, the Real Culprit
Tips for Ego-regulation

Chapter 6: **Power of Concentration** 34
The Honeybee and the Housefly
What Is Concentration?
Benefits of Concentration

Chapter 7: **Sneaky Distractions** 41
Boiling the Milk
Distraction and its Types
Dangers of Distraction

Chapter 8: **Secrets of Focus** 49
Hanuman's Long Jump
Overcoming the Challenges to Stay Focused
Arjuna Wins Draupadi's Hand

SECTION 2: FROM DISTRACTION TO CONCENTRATION **57**

Chapter 1: **Bring the Mind Back** **58**
The Mind Is Like a Kid
Lord Krishna's Attentiveness Formula
Chapter 2: **Practice and Detachment** **63**
Restrain the Restless Mind
Chapter 3: **External and Internal Mind Control** **70**
Out of Sight, Out of Mind!
The Joy of 'Mind Control'
Chapter 4: **Is Multitasking Bad?** **79**
All at Once!
Two Sides of Multitasking
Chapter 5: **Cool Tools for Focused Studies** **87**
Determination for Concentration
Mindfulness Practices
Chapter 6: **Chose the Right Role Models** **97**
Is Popularity the Criteria?
Following and Being a Role Model
Chapter 7: **Smart Use of Smart Phones and Social Media!** **103**
Aditi's Spoiled Test
Making Smart Choices
From Phone to Playground
Uplift Yourself
Chapter 8: **The Ultimate Focus Formula** **113**
Taming the Dog
The Success Story of Universal Creation
The Power of Prayers
A Daily Prayer to Reach Greater Heights

Acknowledgements **120**
About the Author **121**

KNOW your MIND

SECTION 1

Have you ever wondered how your mind works? Why do you feel happy, sad, or excited? How does your body affect your mind, and how does your mind influence your body? Why is it important to keep the mind under control? And what's the difference between the mind, intelligence, and ego?

In this section, we'll explore all these fascinating questions in a fun and simple way. You'll discover the two types of bodies you have—the one you see and the invisible one within. We'll talk about how your desires and emotions arise in your mind and how they shape your actions.

You'll learn how intelligence acts like a guide to keep your mind on the right path and how ego, though important, can sometimes create trouble. We'll also explore the incredible power of focus, why distractions happen, and how to overcome them.

With engaging stories and easy-to-follow tips, this section will help you understand your mind better and use it wisely.

Ready to take a journey into your mind? Let's get started!

1 The Body-dress

Who Am I?

Geethik was a physics teacher who bonded well with his students. One day, he passed a noisy classroom and noticed two kids arguing.

During the argument, one of the kids, Priyanka, said hurtful things to Sapna, calling her a 'fat girl' and asking her to go away. Sapna, feeling upset, responded, 'Why do you comment on me every day? What harm did I do to you?'

To Priyanka's surprise, a third girl stepped in, defending Sapna, 'Priyanka, be mindful of your words. Sapna is my best friend; she is a good person and helps others. You can't be so mean and insult her like this.'

The students, noticing a teacher's presence, became silent and stood up to greet him.

Geethik invited Priyanka to the podium. She was a bit nervous but walked up to him. With a comforting smile, Geethik gently asked, 'What's your name, dear child?'

'Priyanka,' she replied.

'Which standard are you studying in?' he inquired.

'I'm a third grader,' she answered.

'Excellent,' he praised. Pointing at Priyanka's hand, he asked, 'What is this?'

'Hand!' she replied.

'Whose hand is this?' he asked.

'My hand,' she replied with a smile.

'Are you the hand?' he questioned.

'No,' she said.

Geethik then pointed to her leg, asking, 'What is this?'

Priyanka responded, 'It's a leg.'

'Whose leg?' he inquired.

'My leg,' Priyanka replied.

'Are you the leg?' he asked again.

Priyanka giggled and said, 'No.'

Geethik then directed his attention to her head, asking, 'What is this?'

Priyanka answered, 'It's a head.'

'Whose head?' he continued.

'My head,' Priyanka replied.

'Are you the head?' he asked once more.

Priyanka shook her head and said, 'No.'

Finally, he pointed to her uniform and asked, 'What is this?'

Priyanka said, 'It's a school uniform.'

'Whose uniform?' Geethik questioned.

'My uniform,' Priyanka replied.

He smiled and asked, 'Are you the uniform?'

Priyanka laughed and said, 'No!'

'Thank you,' Geethik concluded. 'So, you are not the body!' Turning to the students, he said, 'Little Priyanka is saying this. Not me!'

The children smiled, laughed, and clapped. They were eager for more explanation. Priyanka returned to her desk.

Geethik continued, 'Kids, think of your body like the dress you wear. When you were a tiny baby, you had small clothes, and as you grew, your clothes got bigger, just like your body became taller. But the important thing to remember is that the person inside those clothes is "you", and that "you" doesn't change. The physical body grows from being a baby to a child, then to an adult, and finally, to an elderly person, but the person inside stays the same. That's why we say "my body" and not "I body", just like our friend Priyanka mentioned. It means the body belongs to us, but we are not the body. We are the person inside the body. Do you understand, Priyanka?'

Priyanka replied, 'Yes, sir.'

Geethik continued, 'So, it is not proper behaviour to tease or insult someone based on their bodily attributes. Some bodies are thin, some fat; some tall, some short; some fair, some dark; and so on. We should give more importance to people within these bodies and not judge them based on their looks! That's because the body is just like a covering on the person, similar to your dress. Whether your friend wears a fancy dress or a simple one, you continue to love your friend, right?'

Priyanka understood the lesson. She stood up, looked at Sapna, and said, 'Sorry, Sapna. I have teased you many times. I wouldn't do it again.'

Sapna smiled, and the other children appreciated Priyanka's apology.

Geethik said, 'That's great, Priyanka. Mistakes happen, but good children are those who understand their mistakes, honestly apologize for them, and don't repeat them. From now on, Sapna and you are friends, right?'

Priyanka responded, 'Yes, sir.' Once again, numerous smiles lit up the classroom.

Geethik then concluded, saying, 'But one final caution, children. Although we are not our bodies, it's our responsibility to take care of our bodies properly as long as we live within them. We need to brush our teeth well, take a bath daily, wear clean clothes, eat nutritious food, sleep on time, do some exercise, and cultivate healthy habits to look after the body well.'

That day, the students learned a valuable lesson.

Takeaways from the Tale

- You are not the body, but the person within the body.
- The body is like clothing, changing with time, but the person within remains constant.
- Although we are not the body, we shouldn't act carelessly towards it.
- We should consider our body to be God's gift and look after it so that we can serve others.
- Words hold weight—never comment on someone's appearance and learn to respect others.
- A sincere apology builds bridges and creates understanding and friendship.

The Gita's First Lesson

'The body is temporary and the person inside the body (soul) is eternal. The body is subject to multiple changes but the soul isn't.'

The real you, the person inside the body, is everlasting and doesn't have a beginning or end. This is the first lesson by Lord Krishna in the Bhagavad Gita. It helps us understand that we are more than just our bodies. Here are the Sanskrit verses that convey the vital concepts of the story.

Changing Bodies Is Like Changing Clothes

vāsāṁsi jīrṇāni yathā vihāya
navāni gṛhṇāti naro 'parāṇi
tathā śarīrāṇi vihāya jīrṇāny
anyāni saṁyāti navāni dehī

'Just as a person puts on a new dress, giving up an old one, the soul accepts new bodies, giving up the old ones.'

(Bhagavad Gita 2.22)

Change of Body Is Natural

dehino 'smin yathā dehe
kaumāraṁ yauvanaṁ jarā
tathā dehāntara-prāptir
dhīras tatra na muhyati

'The person within the body passes through childhood to youth to old age of that body and finally passes into another body at the time of death. A wise person is not puzzled by such bodily changes.'

(Bhagavad Gita 2.13)

Understanding that the soul is eternal and the body is temporary is an important lesson for living a balanced life, free from stress.

In this chapter, you learned that your body is different from your true self. But did you know that everyone has two bodies? If you're curious to learn more about the second body, flip forward to the next chapter.

TRY THIS OUT!

PICTURE PARADE

Look for photographs of yourself from the day you were small up until now. Then, on a big chart paper, stick them in ascending order. Observe how your body constantly changes while the person 'you' remains the same!

2 The Tale of Two Bodies

The Mystery of the Invisible Body

On a bright and sunny day, curious nine-year-old Arun approached his wise mom. It was evident that he had a big, burning question on his mind.

'Mom, my friend told me something really strange today. He said we have not one but two bodies! Is that true?'

'Indeed, it's true, my dear,' she replied.

Arun was both puzzled and surprised. He blurted out, 'I've always believed we only have one body. How can we have two? Does everyone have two bodies or just a few lucky ones?'

'Oh, my inquisitive explorer, everyone has two bodies!' exclaimed his mother.

Arun was even more intrigued and said, 'But I've never seen the second one!'

'Our tiny eyes can't see everything. Just because we can't see something doesn't mean it doesn't exist. Many things keep working in the background, silently, unseen by us,' his mother explains.

Arun found his mom's words logical but wasn't completely satisfied.

'You can't see tiny insects and bacteria, but they exist. You can't see the air, but it's there. You can feel the cool breezes and the strong wind, right? Without air, we can't even survive.'

'Got it, Mom. We can't see everything, but it's there. So, what's this invisible second body we all have?' Arun replies.

'Before I tell you, you tell me which of your bodies is visible?'

Arun immediately says, 'My body with hands, legs, head, eyes, ears, and all the fun stuff!'

'Yes, but hidden behind that visible body is the "subtle body", which we can't see. It consists of three things: the mind, intelligence, and ego. In Sanskrit, they're known as manas, buddhi, and ahankara, respectively. Everyone has it, knows about it, and experiences its functions, but we can't see it.'

Arun thoughtfully says, 'I get it. I can't see my mind, although I can see my hands and legs. But I know it's there.'

'Exactly! There's a lot more to learn about the subtle body and its three parts. Let's start with the "mind" or "manas". Do you know how it works?'

Arun replies, 'We think with our mind. It's where all our wishes and thoughts are.'

'Yes! The mind is like a treasure chest filled with thoughts, wishes, feelings, and emotions. Some are positive and some are negative. Your mind holds your thoughts and feelings but can't tell if they're good or bad. It's like an eager, playful puppy; innocent and excited, but it needs guidance.'

'So, who guides it? Teachers and parents, right?' asks Arun.

'Yes, indeed, but they're not always around,' his mom answers. 'So, your "intelligence" or "buddhi" is the superhero that guides your mind. It's the second part of the subtle body. While your mind comes up with desires, your intelligence does the thinking, analysis, reasoning, and decision-making. It's like a wise mentor within you. It helps you choose the right path.'

'Ah, like my inner guide!'

'Exactly! Your intelligence is your compass through the jungle of thoughts in your mind.'

Arun pauses and asks, 'And what's this "ego" you mentioned? I've heard that it can make you proud and look down on others.'

'Ah, the ego is a bit tricky,' his mother says. 'Let me explain the basics of "ahankara" or ego. It means a "sense of identity". People often identify themselves with their roles, positions, status, gender, and more. That's their ego. But all these identities can change. Although temporary, everyone needs to have a sense of identity to function in this world. But it's the ego's "dark side" that can lead to problems like pride or jealousy.'

'So, it's like a character that always wants to be the star in a story?' reflects Arun.

'Yes! Ego can make you think you're the best at everything, not admit when you're wrong, or look down on others. That's called a superiority complex, and it is a function of ego. On the flip side, ego can also make you feel inferior and jealous of those in higher positions, creating an inferiority complex.'

'Wow, it's a lot to take in, Mom.'

'I understand, Arun. It's a heavy topic. But now you know that we all have two bodies—the visible and the invisible.'

'Yes, Mom, a "gross body" and a "subtle body". That's pretty cool!'

'Indeed, it is. Both bodies work together to help us navigate through life, depending on our choices. You're on the path to understanding a deeper part of yourself, my curious explorer.'

Takeaways from the Tale

- We all have two bodies: one visible (gross) and the other invisible (subtle).
- Mind, intelligence, and ego are the three aspects of the subtle body.

The Wonders of the Subtle Body

Our invisible subtle body is a world of wonder, with the mind, intelligence, and ego working together to help us navigate life. By understanding the functions of these elements and with the expert guidance of our elders, we can make better choices in life. Thus, we can channel our emotions and desires in a positive direction.

- **The Mysterious Mind:** Your mind is a storehouse of all your thoughts, desires, emotions, and feelings. The mind is like a bustling city where thoughts roam, memories reside, and emotions sway. Thinking, feeling, and willingness are the functions of the mind, but innocent as it is, the mind can't understand if they are good or bad.
- **The Mighty Intelligence:** Intelligence is that part of the subtle body that does the job of analysing, reasoning, planning, and distinguishing between right and wrong, good and bad, beneficial and harmful. Mind is the one which desires, but intelligence is the decision-maker. It acts as a filter, sorting through your mind's thoughts and emotions.

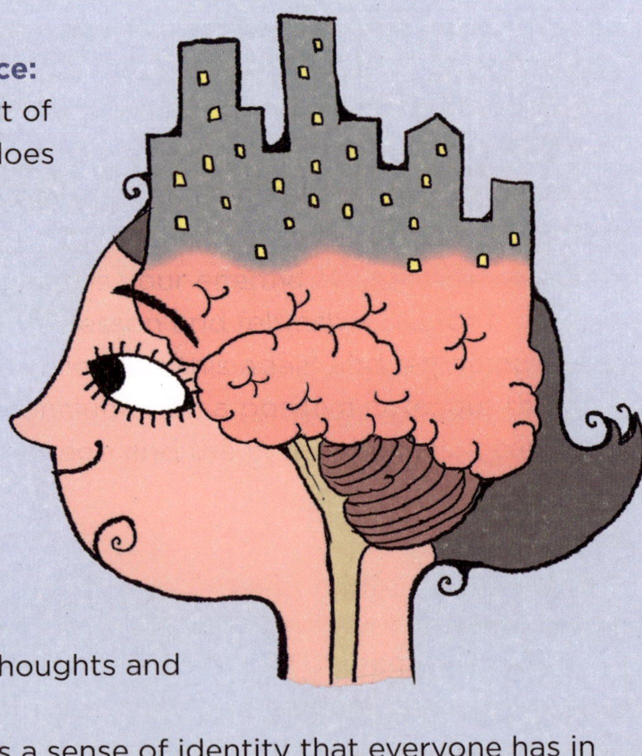

- **The Tricky Ego:** Ego is a sense of identity that everyone has in this world. But the problem comes when one overly identifies with one's position, designation, and status—either high or low. That sense of identity turns into a superiority complex or inferiority complex, or in other words, pride or jealousy that disrupts one's peace of mind and relationships.

Just like a caring friend, our subtle body can help us grow and become the best version of ourselves, provided we get sound guidance. But that same subtle body can get us into trouble if we aren't careful or guided expertly.

We learnt the functions of the mind, intelligence, and ego. But how are these interconnected? How do they influence each other? Where does the mind gather its inputs? Do you want to know how you can be the boss of your mind? The rest of the book elaborates on these subjects along with providing you some cool tools to grow and glow. So why wait? Let's march onward!

TRY THIS OUT!

Look (well, maybe not with your eyes!) around you and write the names of five things whose presence you can feel but cannot see.

3 The Mind's Desires and Emotions

Anu's Desires Fulfilled!

It was 5 p.m. and Anu was eagerly waiting at the school gate for her dad to pick her up. Soon, Anu's dad arrived in a car. She greeted him with a big smile and gave him a warm hug before she got into the car. Dad started driving.

Inquisitive, Anu asked, 'Dad, are we going to the store now?'

'Why the store?' Dad playfully asked.

Anu felt a bit disappointed, and with a pouty face, she said, 'I have been asking you for a few days to buy the shining swan doll.'

Dad smiled and finally agreed, 'All right, we'll check it out on our way home.'

Anu's face lit up with joy, and she said, 'Thank you, Dad! I can't wait! How long will it take to get to the store?'

'About twenty minutes,' Dad replied. 'By the way, where did you see that swan?'

'I saw it at Lalitha's home. She had one, and it was so cute! I want to get an even better one than hers,' Anu shared.

Dad smiled and offered some wisdom, 'Why compare and compete with Lalitha? Be happy with what you have and let her be happy with what she has.'

Anu nodded, taking in the valuable advice.

At the store, Anu was surrounded by numerous swans of different sizes, making it tough to choose. After careful consideration, she picked one. Dad paid for it, and they headed to the vegetarian restaurant nearby.

Excitedly, Anu asked, 'Dad, can I have my favourite strawberry ice cream, please?'

Dad suggested, 'Why not try something refreshing, like fresh fruit juice?

'No, I don't like it. I want ice cream only.'

Dad smiled and got her the ice cream. Anu enjoyed it and finished it quickly. Then, they headed home.

Anu couldn't contain her excitement; she began singing her favourite song, which she had once heard on her dad's phone. It was a tune that accompanied her during her walks, runs, and playtime. When she reached home, the fragrance of incense wafting from their worship room made her smile with satisfaction.

Jumping and smiling, she told her mom, 'Mom, see what Dad got me! I have this beautiful swan! I can't wait to show this to Lalitha!'

Anu claimed her favourite spot at home, a corner seat on the sofa she cherished so much. She wouldn't let anyone else sit there. If someone tried, she'd politely make them stand, and then she would take her place. Now, Anu sat there with her beautiful swan doll in her lap.

Excitement still bubbling, Anu turned to her mom and asked, 'Can you make me some strawberry ice cream at home? It was so yummy at the restaurant!'

Anu's mother, not knowing the recipe, warmly promised to try and learn it. A few days later, after some delightful kitchen adventures, she succeeded. Anu's heart brimmed with happiness.

Anu eagerly showed her new shining swan to her Lalitha and graciously shared the homemade ice cream her mom had perfected. Following her father's wise advice, Anu gradually let go of comparing herself

with Lalitha, and they began playing together happily. It turned out that sharing joys and homemade treats made their friendship even sweeter, creating warm memories that would last a lifetime.

Takeaways from the Tale

OUR MIND:

- Tends to compare and compete with others.
- Produces thoughts and desires when our senses interact with sense objects.
- Creates emotions and feelings when we interact with people around us.

The fulfilment of desires makes the mind happy, while unfulfillment makes it sad.

Have you observed?

Eyes: In this little tale, Anu's eyes were captivated by the beauty of the doll in Lalitha's hand, and she longed to have one just like it. Other toys didn't interest her.

Tongue: Her tongue savoured the delicious strawberry ice cream, and she couldn't help but wish for more. The fruit juice didn't quite match up.

Nose: The sweet fragrance of incense at home held a special place in her mind. Her nose found itself drawn to it, making it her favourite scent.

Ears: Anu's ears were enchanted by the sound of her favourite song, and she couldn't resist humming the same melody repeatedly.

Skin: Her body found comfort in her favourite spot on the sofa, and she yearned to sit there again and again; no other place would do.

Mind: Anu's mind experienced joy whenever she got her favourite things, and her mind faced disappointment when she didn't get what she liked. She also felt encouraged and excited when her parents did what she wanted. She felt disappointed when her father said something against her desires. She also felt a bit competitive with her friend. In this way, each experience etched its mark on her growing mind.

How Do Desires and Emotions Enter Your Mind?

Our five senses—eyes, tongue, nose, ears, and skin—are like our own personal detectives, always on the lookout for interesting things in the world. They find objects like shapes, flavours, scents, sounds, and textures, and when they connect with these things, they create feelings in our minds—some good and some not so good.

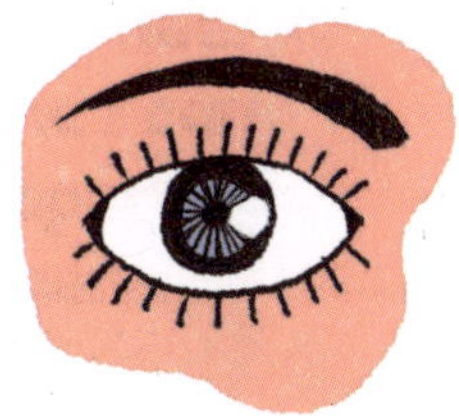

When we see something beautiful or taste something delicious, our minds remember the joy, and we want to experience it again. But if we encounter something scary or unpleasant, our minds store a not-so-happy memory, and we try to avoid it in the future. This happens with sounds too; annoying noises remind our minds to stay away from them next time.

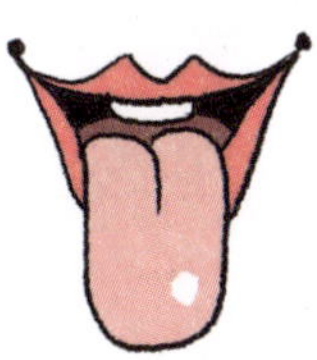

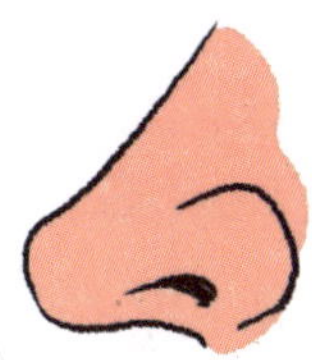

It's not just our senses; the people we interact with also play a big role in how we feel. Our interactions with people around us can give rise to various emotions and feelings in our minds. Those emotions include happiness, sadness, excitement, anger, gratitude, disgust, and so on. These feelings are natural and are sometimes pleasant and sometimes unpleasant. Positive emotions make us feel joyful and content, while negative ones can sometimes lead to stress or distress.

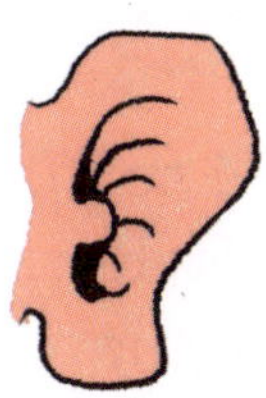

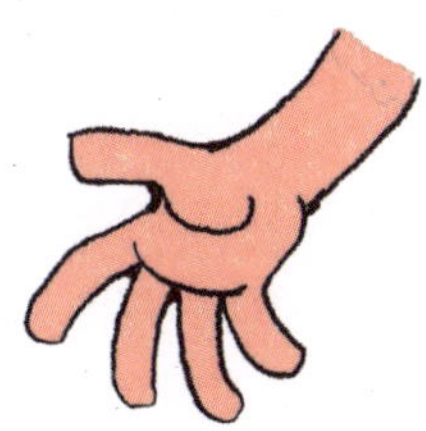

So, our minds gather lots of memories through our senses and interactions, creating thoughts, desires, and emotions. Sometimes we feel happy, and sometimes we feel sad.

To stay away from stress and distractions, we need to be careful about what we expose our senses to.

How Does the Mind Influence the Body?

Our mind can make our body do lots of things! For example, when you think about eating something tasty like a rasgulla, your mind tells your body to do multiple things, such as using your eyes to find the sweet shop, moving your legs to get there, giving the shopkeeper the money to purchase the sweet by using your hands, and finally, savouring the yummy treat. This is how your mind makes your body and senses perform tasks to reach the goal!

It's good to enjoy things you love, but in excess, it's a bad idea. For instance, sometimes, our mind wants more than our tummy can handle, like wanting to eat lots of gulab jamuns even when we're already full. That's when we need to tell our minds, 'Hey, eating too many sweets is not good for me.'

The next question is who will tell this to the mind? Who will control the mind's thoughts, desires, emotions, and feelings, especially when they go in the wrong direction? To find an answer to this secret, simply flip forward to the next chapter!

TRY THIS OUT!

Bring a piece of candy, a slice of lime, a slice of bitter gourd, and some table salt. Now taste each one of these items and notice how your mind responds as your tongue experiences a change of flavour. Observe the connection between your mind and senses.

4 Intelligence: The Mind's Friend

Control the Kite of Your Mind

One day, in a fifth-grade classroom, the math teacher noticed Raj peeping through the window. She didn't say anything but kept watching him from time to time. After a while she noticed him sketching a bus in his notebook. In a few moments, he started pulling his classmate into a conversation, disturbing him and preventing him from listening to the class. Raj would watch the wall clock every few minutes. He seemed like a hyperactive puppy, leaping from one stray thought to another.

After the class, the teacher called Raj and asked him about his lack of concentration during the class. Raj didn't have an explanation, but surely, he realized that his mind had been distracted. The teacher mildly told him to be more focused.

That day, Raj's friend, Madhu, met him. Raj said, 'Madhu, my mind is as wild as a tornado! It's restless like a squirrel on a sugar rush. The distant hum of traffic outside my classroom suddenly transports me to imaginary journeys through crowded streets. Seeing the vibrant illustrations in my textbooks, I fall into daydreams. The distractions in my mind are visible in my body language. Today my teacher warned me about my behaviour in the classroom.'

Madhu chuckled and said, 'Raj, I understand. Minds can be trickier than the wind. But let's try something fun.'

Madhu gave Raj a kite and asked him to fly it. Raj held the string of the kite tightly and allowed the kite to fly high. He kept a good watch on the movements of the wind and accordingly pulled and released the string of the kite. Initially anxious that the wind might break the kite, he made sure to hold the string carefully. Soon, his kite was high above, soaring in the sky, unharmed by the wind. He looked happily at Madhu.

Madhu smiled back and said, 'All your thoughts induced by things and people around you are like the wind. The kite is like your mind. And the string you are holding is like your intelligence. If you don't hold the string properly and don't control its movements in a balanced way, your kite won't fly high. It could even be lost and destroyed. So, the key is to use the string wisely!'

Raj was impressed and curious to know more. Madhu continued, 'Just like you adjust the string, pulling and releasing it carefully to keep the kite steady, you can learn to calm your mind by sharpening your intelligence. To protect your mind from the wild wind of thoughts, desires, and visual impressions, you need to develop sound intelligence.'

Raj asked, 'But how do I sharpen my intelligence?'

Madhu replied, 'You can do it in two ways: one, by reading wisdom texts and two, by hearing from wise and experienced people. You need to understand what's right and wrong for you. And just like Rome wasn't built in one day, you can't achieve complete mind control in an instant. By enhancing your intelligence, you can control your mind gradually.'

Raj practised what Madhu said. Raj went home and consulted his grandfather about the matter. He recommended reading the sixth chapter of the Bhagavad Gita, where Lord Krishna described the art of mind control. Whenever Raj had doubts, his grandfather would clarify them lovingly. He started to understand what was good and bad for him, and gradually Raj's mind settled. He realized that with practice and patience, even the wildest minds could find peace, just like a kite finding a calm spot in the windy sky.

Takeaways from the Tale

- The mind is restless and tends to wander everywhere with random thoughts.
- Intelligence can regulate the distractions of the mind.
- Intelligence can be sharpened by reading wisdom texts and associating oneself with wise people.

Hierarchy of Elements in Our Bodies

So far, we explored the different components of our inner self: the subtle mind, intelligence, and ego to some extent. We also looked at how these elements are connected to our physical body and its five senses. Now, let's delve deeper into their relationships and hierarchy, as elucidated by Lord Krishna in the Bhagavad Gita (3.42):

indriyāṇi parāṇy āhur
indriyebhyaḥ paraṁ manaḥ
manasas tu parā buddhir
yo buddheḥ paratas tu saḥ

'Mind is higher than the senses. Intelligence is superior to the mind. Higher than the intelligence is the self (the person).'

Bhagavad Gita (3.42)

In our inner world, intelligence plays the role of a knowledgeable captain who directs the ship of our mind and senses. A harmonious coordination among these components under the wise leadership of intelligence is crucial for navigating the ocean of life effectively.

The Body Chariot

To make this idea of intelligence as the leader of our inner world even simpler, the ancient wisdom texts give us an interesting analogy.

Imagine your body as a chariot! It's like a magical chariot driven by five horses. Each horse represents one of your senses—eyes, ears, nose, tongue, and skin. These horses are trying to run towards different destinations of sight, sound, smell, taste, and touch, respectively. The charioteer represents your intelligence and its reins, the mind. Just as the chariot driver holds the reins and controls the movements of the horses, your intelligence guides your mind and senses.

And guess who's the passenger in this amazing chariot? That's you! You're the one travelling on this chariot.

Just like a skilled charioteer directs the horses with the reins, your intelligence is there to guide your mind and senses on the exciting adventure of life. So remember, as you travel through life's experiences, your intelligence is your trusted guide, steering you in the right direction.

The First Mindfulness Tip

Now imagine a scenario where the ropes are weak, the driver isn't strong enough to manage the reins, and the five horses of the chariot end up running in different directions. What do you think would happen? The chariot might get into an accident and end up in a muddy ditch. Certainly, it won't reach where it's supposed to. To reach the intended destination, the driver should be capable of controlling the ropes and horses efficiently.

Similarly, in our life journey, we have certain goals to attain. And our body is the most important tool to attain those goals. If our bodily senses, like wild horses, are constantly chasing after the sense objects of seeing, hearing, touching, tasting, and smelling; and if our mind is always distracted, being pulled in various directions, reaching our goals becomes a challenge. So, what's the solution? The driver has to be fit and able i.e. our intelligence needs to be sharp enough to regulate the mind and the senses. It's our responsibility to use our sharp intelligence to regulate and guide our minds, ensuring that we stay on a path that is safe and beneficial for our well-being.

Sharpening your intelligence is vital for sense control and mind control.

Congrats! Now you know how your intelligence and mind are related. But did you know there is another boss who secretly directs all the activities of the mind? Curious to find out who it is? Then flip forward!

TRY THIS OUT!

STEP 1: The Treasure Chest of the Mind

Decorate a box, and fill it with colourful paper cutouts representing your various wishes, thoughts, and emotions.

STEP 2: The Sorting Game of Intelligence

Take two new empty boxes and mark '+' and '–' on them. Now take a chit from the mind box, and start analysing your wish or feeling that you have written on it. If you find it to be positive, put it in the box marked with '+', and if you if it is negative, drop it in the box marked with '-'. Thus, by using your intelligence, you can understand how many positive and negative thoughts or feelings your mind holds.

STEP 3: Peer Review

Call your close friend, and ask them to do Step 2 for you. Now compare the way you and your friend analysed various emotions and desires.

5 Ego: The Mind's Boss

Two Friends Who Became Enemies

Dev was a young son of a wealthy businessman. An experienced adviser would guide Dev's father in his business. The adviser wasn't so wealthy but hardworking and intelligent. He had a son named Adi who was a good friend of Dev's.

One day, Dev, Adi, and a few other boys decided to go on an exciting picnic to a lovely farm. The farm was filled with trees with colourful and sweet-smelling flowers, tasty fruits, and the joyful melodies of singing birds and buzzing bumblebees. There was a beautiful lake filled with lotuses. The centre of attraction of the farm was a gorgeous stone temple that had breathtaking architecture. The boys enjoyed themselves in the new place.

It was lunchtime, and all the boys were called for their meals in a big hall where there were no dining tables. They had to leave their footwear outside the hall, sit down on straw mats, and eat their meals on banana leaf plates. It was fun and many boys liked the experience, although some found it a bit austere.

Dev and Adi chatted for a long time during their meals. After a while, they realized that it was already time for the next event of the day. They finished their meals, and hurriedly came out of the hall and started wearing their shoes. However, in the rush, Adi accidentally wore Dev's shoes.

Dev became very upset when he noticed this. He scolded Adi, 'Adi, why did you wear my shoes? I belong to a wealthy businessman's family, and I am higher in status than you. You are like my servant. You should know your place. Your father is just an employee of my father. You are living on the salary we give you. Still, you dare to wear my expensive shoes!'

Upon hearing Dev's harsh words, Adi became angry and retorted, 'You talk big, but you don't even know your place! Aren't business people like you dependent on expert advisers like us for your success? Your wealth is nothing but what your ancestors have gained. My father is a hard worker. Although our ancestors weren't wealthy, my father, with his great intelligence, reached this position. Without my father's advice, your father cannot flourish in his business.'

Adi's words severely hurt Dev.

In a fit of rage, Adi not only scolded Dev but snatched away his shoes and pushed him into the lake before heading home. Later, someone rescued Dev from the lake, and he narrated the incident to his father. Dev's father, angered by the mistreatment of his son, decided to take the matter to his business adviser to seek justice and settle the grievance.

The adviser, feeling regretful, spoke, 'Sir, your son has insulted my son, who then behaved in this way. I apologize for my son's behaviour.'

The businessman said, 'I understand. You need not be sorry.'

He then turned to the two boys and said, 'Dear children, although you both are good friends apparently, each of you unconsciously thought of yourself better than the other. You identified yourself too much with your fathers' positions and developed a false ego. My adviser and I are good friends. Although we have our positions in the hierarchy, we respect each other for what we are and you both should also be like that. Don't allow envy, pride, and arrogance to disrupt your sweet friendship. Learn to respect each other, and get rid of this false ego which is your enemy.'

The two boys understood the lesson and felt ashamed for their misbehaviour. They never quarrelled like this again and remained good friends. Thankfully, the story concluded on a positive note, but this incident highlights the power of ego and the consequences it can bring.

Takeaways from the Tale

- Pride induces one into such petty quarrels even with friends.
- Momentary ego clashes can make even friends into lifelong enemies.
- Overly identifying oneself with our positions makes us look down upon others.

False Ego, the Real Culprit

As we've talked about earlier, ego is like a 'sense of identity.'

In life, we all have different roles, such as a student, a teacher, a doctor, an engineer, or a scientist. These roles are natural and important in the world. It's absolutely fine to feel happy about our good positions, talents, and achievements. This is what we call a 'healthy identity'.

However, problems arise when we become too attached to these temporary roles, titles, and accomplishments. This excessive identification with external elements can lead to distorted mentalities, such as feeling inferior or superior to others. In simpler terms, it can cause envy and pride. This is what we refer to as an 'unhealthy ego' or 'false ego'.

Striking a balance between acknowledging our achievements and not letting them define us is key to maintaining a healthy sense of self-confidence.

False ego manifests itself in many shades like self-obsession, self-righteousness, selfishness, arrogance, harsh speech, insensitivity, domination, and so on.

Unhealthy Ego

Imagine a boy who excels in his exams; it's normal for him to feel happy about his success. However, if he becomes too attached to this achievement and starts looking down on classmates with lower scores, he develops a sense of superiority or pride. This is an example of the false ego in action. This false pride disrupts his relationships with his classmates.

Now, if this boy doesn't maintain the top position in the next exams, he might feel disappointed, discouraged, and frustrated. The same person who once felt a sense of superiority may now experience an inferiority complex. This is how the false ego operates.

On the flip side, if the student doesn't let the title of 'first ranker' get to his head and instead maintains good relationships with all classmates, even helping them with their studies, he can build strong and positive friendships. This approach not only keeps the ego in check but also fosters a supportive and harmonious environment.

How Is the Mind Connected to Ego?

The mind is subordinate to ego. The mind's role is to think, desire, and feel. If an egoistic student identifies himself with his position as the 'first ranker', his mind thinks, desires and feels according to that position! If a humble student feels himself as a friend of his classmates, his mind thinks, feels and desires to be friendly with fellow students, irrespective of his scores and ranks.

In summary, *the mind follows ego*. And if we can mould our egos not to overly identify with one's positions, designation, and roles, the innocent mind becomes our friend. So, the key is to focus on taming our ego and being kind to others.

Tips for Ego-regulation

1. **Analyse:** When we develop good intelligence, we can even analyse the functions of the false ego, and regulate it.
2. **Seek help:** Sometimes, our false ego is difficult to understand, and we can't detect how it is fooling us and disrupting our relations. At that time, mature well-wishers can help us, because their good intelligence is superior to our false ego.

Examples of a Healthy Ego

'I'm happy about my achievements and feel good about my hard work.'
'I believe in my abilities and know that I can learn from my mistakes.'
'I'm confident in my skills, and I enjoy helping others when I can.'
'I'm happy for my friends when they do well, and I like to celebrate their successes.'
'I know that I'm unique, and I value the things that make me special.'
'I'm comfortable with who I am and accept myself, flaws and all.'

Examples of an Unhealthy Ego

'I'm better than everyone else at everything, and no one can match up to me.'

'If I make a mistake, I'm a total failure, and I can never do anything right.'

'I don't need help from anyone; I can handle everything on my own.'

'I can't stand the success of my friends, and I don't want to see them do well.'

'I pretend to be someone I'm not just to fit in with certain groups.'

'I'm always trying to be perfect, and I can't accept any of my flaws.'

It's essential to maintain a healthy balance between self-confidence and humility.

Now that we've equipped ourselves with knowledge about our invisible body, let's dive into the next chapter and discover the art of concentration. This powerful skill can help us stay focused on our march towards success. So, let's move on!

TRY THIS OUT!

Identify which of the above statements suits you. Did you realize why the statements in the 'Healthy Ego' category promote a balanced sense of identity? Did you understand why the statements in the 'Unhealthy Ego' category can lead to problems and unhappiness? Share your thoughts about these statements with your friends and parents.

The Ego *Mask: Create* masks representing various shades of healthy and unhealthy ego—like happiness and pride, confidence and arrogance, etc. You and your friends can wear the masks and have a conversation with supporting arguments that reflect what your masks represent.

6 Power of Concentration

The Honeybee and the Housefly

Once upon a time, in a lush and colourful garden, there lived a busy little housefly. The housefly was always distracted, buzzing from one place to another, and never staying still for a moment. He couldn't help himself because everything in the garden was so fascinating!

One sunny morning, the housefly decided to explore the garden like never before. He flew everywhere and zoomed around, his tiny wings making a soft humming sound. He saw beautiful flowers, butterflies fluttering by, and even a sparkling fountain. Then, he moved on to exploring the litter in the dustbin. It was full of leftovers and all sorts of things that interested him. He dived right in, buzzing around and inspecting every crumb and piece of garbage.

As the housefly was lost in his explorations, he heard a gentle voice behind him. It was a graceful honeybee. She was flying near a lovely flower, sipping nectar with great focus.

The housefly said, 'Hey there, Ms Bee! Why are you stuck to a single flower? There's so much to explore in this garden and you're missing out on all the exciting things! I couldn't resist all these fascinating crumbs and leftovers in this dustbin. There's so much to see and taste!'

The honeybee continued to sip the sweet nectar, not the least bit distracted by the housefly's excitement.

Then Ms Bee said, 'I understand your curiosity, Mr Fly. But do you know that when I stick to a flower and focus on sipping its nectar, I can collect the sweetest and most delicious nectar from that flower? The pleasure I get from one flower is way greater than what you get from roaming about the whole garden. It's like a treasure hidden inside each one. Plus, I help the garden grow by spreading pollen from one flower to another.'

Housefly was impressed. 'I see. So, you're like a guardian of the flowers. That's pretty cool!'

'Yes,' the honeybee replied. 'And you can be a guardian of your adventures, too, by practising concentration, instead of being distracted by everything that you see.'

The housefly thought for a moment, grasping the honeybee's perspective. He understood that he, too, could enrich his adventures through focus rather than distraction—like Ms Honeybee who concentrated on one flower and enjoyed its nectar. The honeybee obtained extraordinary nectar and much more by concentrating on a single flower, something the housefly missed despite discovering many more places in the garden.

From that day forward, the housefly aimed to combine his curiosity and focus. By doing so, he discovered that the world had so much more to offer when he gave his complete attention to each moment and experience. Like the honeybee, he realized that concentrating on one thing at a time enhanced his adventures and made them even more thrilling.

Takeaways from the Tale

- When you don't concentrate on one thing, you are distracted by everything.
- Balancing curiosity with concentration leads to meaningful discoveries.
- Being present in the moment enriches life's adventures.
- Concentration helps you and allows you to help others as well.

What Is Concentration?

'Concentration' is the mind's ability to focus on a specific task or idea, while ignoring all distractions or unrelated thoughts.

Like when you're reading an interesting book, and you're so absorbed in the story that you don't notice what's happening around you, concentration helps you do better in school, in sports, and in all the fun things you like to do. So, when you're studying, playing a game, or listening to a story, try to use your power of concentration, and you'll do really well.

In the Bhagavad Gita, Lord Krishna says that successful people are those who have a sharp focus on their goals, while unsuccessful people get distracted by many things. Here is verse (2.41) in which He reveals this important art of focus.

vyavasāyātmikā buddhir
ekeha kuru-nandana
bahu-śākhā hy anantāś ca
buddhayo 'vyavasāyinām

'Those who are determined to attain their purpose, focus on one goal. But the intelligence of those who are not determined to attain one goal is diverted towards so many things.'

(Bhagavad Gita 2.41)

So, remember to build good concentration, and you'll be on your way to achieving your goals!

Benefits of Concentration

Concentration is a critical mental skill that plays a vital role in various aspects of our lives. It helps us in:

- **Improved Learning:** Whether studying for an exam, learning a new skill, or grasping a complex concept, concentration is essential. It allows you to absorb and retain information effectively.
- **Enhanced Productivity:** Concentration enables you to work efficiently and complete tasks more accurately and quickly. When we concentrate on a task, we're less likely to make mistakes and more likely to produce good work.
- **Problem Solving:** Concentration helps in analysing problems and coming up with creative and logical solutions. When you concentrate on a problem, your mind can explore different angles and possibilities.
- **Achieving Goals:** To achieve long-term goals, you need to stay focused and work consistently. Concentration helps maintain your commitment to your objectives and attain the fulfilment of those objectives.
- **Reducing Stress:** When you concentrate on the present moment and the task at hand, it can reduce anxiety and stress related to worrying about the past or the future.

Developing concentration is like developing a superpower that helps us perform the most difficult tasks in short periods of time. Do you know who is the enemy of concentration? The answer is distraction. To know what distraction does to you, read the next chapter.

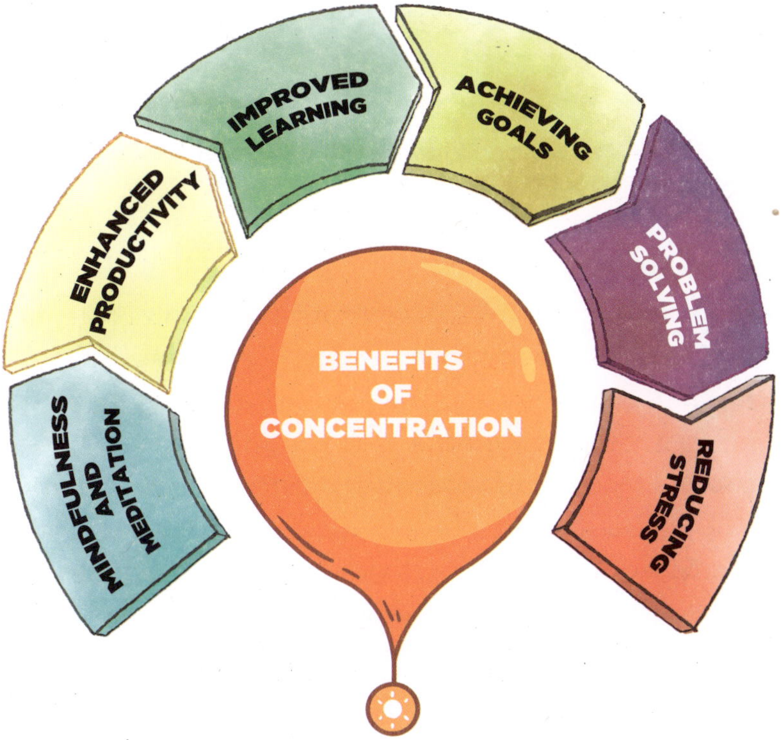

TRY THIS OUT!

Activity: Memory Tray Challenge

Materials: A small tray and various small objects (key, coin, toy, etc.)

Instructions:

Step 1: Place any 5–10 objects on the tray.

Step 2: Observe the objects for 1–2 minutes.

Step 3: Cover the tray and then list as many objects as you remember.

Step 4: Uncover, compare your list, and note what you missed.

Step 5: Add more objects gradually for a greater challenge.

Step 6: Practise regularly and see your memory skills shine!

Enjoy the Memory Tray Challenge!

7 Sneaky Distractions

Boiling the Milk

'Neeta, can you boil the milk for me? It should take around ten minutes,' Mom asked Neeta one sunny Sunday. Neeta was happy to assist her mom with household chores on the weekend.

Mom went to the market, leaving Neeta in charge. Neeta turned on the stove and put the pot of milk on it. She set a timer for ten minutes to make sure everything went smoothly. However, a few minutes into the task, Neeta's phone started buzzing with messages. She thought, 'Oh, my friends are chatting! I'll quickly reply and then get back to the milk.'

To be safe, Neeta turned off the stove and was engrossed in her phone for a short while. Later, she returned to the kitchen and turned the stove back on.

After a few minutes, the doorbell rang. 'Oh, someone's at the door!' Neeta exclaimed and turned off the stove again. She hurried to answer it and had a chat with the neighbour.

She came back to turn on the stove, but just then, her grandma called, and Neeta had to turn off the stove for the third time.

After talking with her grandma, Neeta finally returned to the kitchen and started the flame again, thinking that she had already heated the milk for five minutes, although with some breaks in between. Then she thought, 'Why should I just stand here watching the milk for the next five minutes? I could play a video game.'

Neeta stood next to the stove and started playing the game on her phone. She quickly advanced through the levels, becoming more and more excited as she cleared each step. Finally, she reached a climax point in the game. But as she focused on her game, the milk reached its boiling point and began to spill over. Unfortunately, Neeta didn't realize it, so engrossed was she in her game.

Suddenly, the smell of the boiling milk caught her attention. She grew anxious, but by the time she turned off the flame, half of the milk had already spilt out of the pot.

Neeta's mom returned home. She saw the timer indicating forty-five minutes and the spilt milk. She realized what had happened. She didn't scold her daughter but decided to use this as a valuable teaching moment.

Mom explained, 'Neeta, you were distracted multiple times and you kept turning off the stove. That's why it took so long.'

Neeta, realizing her mistake, admitted, 'Yes, Mom. I got carried away with my phone, the doorbell, a phone call, and my game. I was distracted.'

Mom gently advised her, 'It's important to focus on one task at a time. It makes you more efficient and helps you complete things quickly. Now, let's boil this milk together.'

Together, they concentrated on boiling the milk efficiently and finished it within ten minutes.

Neeta's mother added, 'See, it didn't take so long when we focused, did it? But when we divide our attention among many different things, we can't do justice to any of them. So, it's better to focus on one thing at a time.'

With a wide grin on her face, Neeta promised, 'You're right, Mom. I'll remember to concentrate on each task and not get distracted from now on. Although some distractions are inevitable, staying focused helps you make the most of your time and tasks.'

From that day forward, Neeta tried to be a more attentive and efficient little chef.

Takeaways from the Tale

- Distractions are inevitable but not unavoidable when we are focused.
- Focused attention enhances task efficiency.
- Distractions can lead to mistakes and oversights.
- Effective time management is crucial for task completion.
- Learning from mistakes contributes to personal growth.
- Commitment to improvement leads to positive changes.

Distraction and its Types

'Distraction' is when something unexpectedly takes your attention away from what you're supposed to be doing or thinking about.

In a world full of attractive and misleading things, it can be really hard to focus on our work. With the constant beeping of social media updates and phone conversations, it is tough to concentrate on other activities. Smartphones become doorways to many distractions, affecting our concentration. We use smartphones to stay CONNECTED with everything. But we could get DISCONNECTED from our purpose.

In the Gita, Lord Krishna explains how even smart people's minds can get distracted because of their restless senses:

yatato hy api kaunteya
puruṣasya vipaścitaḥ
indriyāṇi pramāthīni
haranti prasabhaṁ manaḥ

'The senses are so strong and restless that they forcefully drag away the mind even of wise people who know what is right and what is wrong, even if they are trying hard to control the senses.'
(Bhagavad Gita 2.56)

Broadly speaking, there are two kinds of distractions that we tend to succumb to:

1. **External distractions**
2. **Internal distractions**

External distractions come from outside sources, like when you're trying to study physics, and your friend starts telling you about a quarrel they had and you can't help but listen.

Internal distractions come from within ourselves, like when you're studying, but your eyes land on your cricket bat, and your mind pushes you to play a game even though you have an exam tomorrow.

The following is a small list of distractions:

- **Gadgets:** Excessive use of smartphones, tablets, and video games can divert your attention from studies, leading to reduced academic performance, disrupted sleep patterns, and decreased physical activity and personal interactions.
- **Excessive use of TV and Social Media:** Scrolling through social media platforms can consume a significant amount of time if used without keeping a watch on our time. This can cause you to lose focus on your studies, and miss out on essential social interactions in real life. Watching TV shows can lead to procrastination, impacting homework completion and the development of important time management skills.

- **Daydreaming:** Imagine that you're sitting in class and your teacher is explaining a fascinating science experiment. Suddenly, your mind drifts off and starts thinking about your upcoming birthday party. Daydreaming doesn't allow you to pay attention to the lesson.
- **Noisy Environments:** Background noise or disruptive surroundings can make it challenging to concentrate on the task at hand, resulting in reduced productivity and comprehension.
- **Peer Conflicts:** Issues with friends can sometimes preoccupy your mind, affecting your emotional well-being and focus on schoolwork.
- **Lack of Organization:** Poor organization skills can lead to misplaced assignments, forgotten deadlines, and increased stress over incomplete tasks. Moreover, not keeping your room and surroundings clean can distract you with several visual impressions that don't allow you to focus on your work.
- **Health Issues:** Physical and mental health concerns, such as illness, and anxiety, can significantly impact your ability to concentrate and learn effectively. Such problems often require special attention and support.

So, we need to try our best and keep ourselves away from these distractions.

Dangers of Distraction

Frequent distractions can hinder our learning and academic performance. They can result in poor time management and lower grades, impacting our ability to achieve our potential in the activities we choose to pursue. Here are a few dangers we can run into because of distractions:

- **Homework Takes Longer:** When you get distracted, it can take a lot more time to finish your homework. For example, a task that should have taken thirty minutes might take an hour because you kept getting distracted by other things.

- **Making Mistakes:** Distractions can lead to making mistakes. For instance, when you're colouring a picture and someone distracts you, you might accidentally colour outside the lines.
- **Frustration:** Feeling frustrated can be a result of distractions. You may feel annoyed when you can't concentrate because you want to get something done.
- **Learning Challenges:** In school, distractions can make it harder to learn new things. If you're thinking about your favourite video game during a math lesson, you might miss out on important concepts.

By recognizing distractions and learning how to manage them—like finding a quiet place to do your homework—you can improve in school, enjoy your playtime, and enjoy your day. The journey from distraction to concentration begins with identifying what pulls your attention away. But, according to the previous Gita verse, even Lord Krishna acknowledges that even wise and disciplined individuals can face distractions. So, how do we protect ourselves from these disruptions?

TRY THIS OUT!

Distraction Dodge

Objective:

Illustrate the dangers of distractions on performance.

Instructions:

***Assign Tasks**:* Give your friend a simple task (e.g. solving a math problem, or writing a paragraph).

***Introduce Distractions**:* While they work, throw in distractions (e.g. random noises, questions).

***Set a Timer**:* Limit each task to a short time frame (five minutes), and start the clock.

***Reflect**:* Discuss the impact of distractions on task completion and stress levels.

***Group Discussion**:* Share insights on handling distractions and lessons learned.

***Discussion Questions**:*

How did distractions affect your performance?

What strategies helped or hindered your focus?

What can we learn about real-life distractions from this activity?

(Note: Play this game and vice versa i.e. first you throw distractions on your friend and then let your friend test your concentration powers!)

8 Secrets of Focus

Hanuman's Long Jump

Mother Sita, the wife of Lord Rama, had been abducted by the evil king of the demons, Ravana, who held her captive in his golden city of Lanka. To rescue her, Lord Rama dispatched the mighty vanara hero, Hanuman, along with a host of monkey soldiers.

To reach Lanka, Hanuman faced the daunting task of crossing a vast ocean. With unwavering devotion, he climbed a mountain and took the name of Lord Rama, soaring through the sky with immense energy. As he flew, the heavenly gods watched in admiration, showering him with flowers. Recognizing Hanuman's noble mission, Surya, the sun god, softened his rays to keep him cool, while Vayu, the wind god and Hanuman's father, sent gentle breezes to aid his journey.

As Hanuman travelled through the sky, Samudra, the ocean god, wanted to help him. He then called Mainaka, a great mountain, hiding in the depths of the ocean, to assist Hanuman. To prevent Hanuman from getting tired, Mainaka rose from the ocean, covered in trees and vines, shining like a bright star. Hanuman, flying fast, saw this great mountain rise.

At first, Hanuman thought Mainaka was an obstacle and struck it with his chest. Mainaka, the mountain god, then appeared in a human form, stood on the summit of the mountain, and greeted Hanuman. 'O mighty Vanara! You are on a great journey. Please land on my peak and rest for some time. I have delicious fruits and roots for you. Please allow me to serve you.'

Hanuman felt grateful but denied the offer, 'Thank you for your kindness, but I must keep moving. I have an important promise to fulfil, and I don't have time to rest and relax.' Hanuman then gently touched the mountain in appreciation and continued on his journey. The ocean and Mainaka watched him with admiration, wishing him all success.

The heavenly gods (devatas), watching Hanuman, decided to test his strength and intelligence. They called upon Surasa, the mother of the nagas (snakes), to create a challenge for him. Surasa then took on a frightening form and blocked Hanuman's path, saying, 'O Vanara, you have to enter my mouth! I will eat you!'

Hanuman, brave and calm, replied, 'I am on a mission to find Sita, who was taken by demon Ravana. Please let me complete my task.'

Surasa insisted, 'You must enter my mouth now! I received a boon from Lord Brahma, the creator of the universe, that whoever comes in front of me will enter my mouth.'

Hanuman said, 'I must honour the words of Lord Brahma, and I will return soon after

completing my mission and then enter your mouth. Please let me go now.'

But Surasa didn't leave Hanuman. She opened her huge mouth, ready to swallow him. But Hanuman was clever. He grew to a giant size, but Surasa kept making her mouth larger. Hanuman expanded his body, becoming bigger and bigger. Simultaneously, Surasa enlarged her mouth. This competition continued for a while.

At one moment, Hanuman quickly shrank down to the size of a thumb, entered Surasa's mouth, and came out just as fast before she could swallow him. He said, 'I have entered, as you asked! Now, may I go?' Surasa was impressed by Hanuman's cleverness and allowed him to continue his journey.

As Hanuman continued, he was spotted by Simhika, a shape-shifting demoness. She had a magical power using which she could pull people by holding on to their shadows. Thus, she started to pull Hanuman down. Feeling a strange force, Hanuman saw Simhika. At once, he entered her mouth, ripped apart her body, and came out as a hero. Having defeated Simhika, Hanuman continued on his mission and successfully landed in Lanka to fulfil his mission.

The celestial gods cheered for Hanuman's bravery. They said, 'O mighty Vanara! You have shown great courage, skill, and focus towards achieving your goal. Anyone who has these qualities will succeed in their tasks.'

With his heart set on fulfilling his duty, Hanuman found Mother Sita and gave her the hope she had been longing for. Together, they would pave the way for Lord Rama's victory, proving that with determination and courage, even the mightiest challenges can be overcome.

Overcoming the Challenges to Stay Focused

Just as Hanuman faced so many obstacles and challenges on his way to Lanka, we will also face some obstacles in attaining our goals. Taking inspiration from mighty Hanuman, let's overcome those obstacles with care and courage, keeping complete focus on our goals, and finally, attaining them. We all have different challenges to face. But here we see

Takeaways from the Tale

- Don't be allured by temptations and be focused on your goal.
- Know when to prioritize your mission over comfort.
- Use cleverness to solve challenges instead of relying solely on physical strength.
- Courage and patience can overcome even the toughest obstacles.
- Bravery, intelligence, and unwavering focus lead to success.

how Hanuman overcame the challenges of the mind and ego by using his intelligence and emerging successful.

1. **The Mountain of Comfort:** When the goal is yet to be achieved and when you have less time, you can't take undue breaks, rest, or relax. It's easy to get distracted by things that seem nice, comforting, and apparently reasonable. Remember Hanuman's determination to stay focused on his mission when Mainaka presented the opportunity to serve. Hanuman defeated the mind's temptation to receive comfort by intelligently focusing on his mission.
2. **Practise Mindful Gratitude:** Sometimes, we can't accept the support that others offer us, yet we can express gratitude. Hanuman thanked Mainaka for the offer, showing us the importance of appreciating and acknowledging kindness, even if we choose to move on.

3. **Stay Calm and Composed:** When faced with challenges, it's important not to lose composure. Hanuman's ability to think clearly and be mindful of his mission helped him overcome Surasa's test.
4. **Be Clever and Humble:** Hanuman had respect for the boon given by Lord Brahma to Surasa, yet he had to focus on his service to Lord Rama. When we are pulled in different directions, we get emotional and lose our ability to think intelligently. But Hanuman, instead of losing his temper or becoming emotional, cleverly dealt with and satisfied Surasa without obstructing his mission.
5. **Avoid Egoistic Competition:** Hanuman didn't get into an egoistic competition with Surasa. When she was expanding her mouth, he started enlarging his body, but at one point he realized that his purpose wasn't to prove himself to be better than Surasa, but to serve Lord Rama. Sometimes, our ego and obsession to win over others results in unnecessary competition and make us lose focus on our mission. We must strive to avoid it.

6. **Let Go of Negative Feelings:** Simhika represents negativity that can hold us back. Hanuman teaches us that to move forward, we need to let go of fear and negativity, making space for positive thoughts.

These are some powerful lessons we can learn from Hanuman's story. Now, let's explore another story of Arjuna before moving forward!

Arjuna Wins Draupadi's Hand

In the kingdom of Panchala, King Drupada organized a grand swayamvara, a ceremony where eligible suitors could win the hand of his daughter, Draupadi. She was known for her beauty, wisdom, and strength of character. Many kings and warriors gathered to compete for her hand, eager to prove their skills.

The challenge set by King Drupada was a test of archery. In the centre of the arena, a wooden fish was hung from a tall pole. To win Draupadi's hand, a suitor had to shoot an arrow at the fish, but there was a twist: the fish would be spinning, and the archer had to aim at its reflection in a pool of water below. This task required great skill and concentration.

Among the suitors were many powerful kings and great warriors. However, among them was Arjuna, one of the five Pandavas, who had been living in disguise with his brothers in the forest. When the time for the competition arrived, Arjuna knew he had to seize this opportunity.

As the challenge began, each suitor took his turn. Many attempted to shoot the arrow, but none could hit the target. The crowd buzzed with excitement and disappointment as each warrior failed to hit the spinning fish. Some became frustrated, while others tried to show off their strength but missed the mark.

Finally, it was Arjuna's turn. He stepped forward confidently, despite being in disguise. He silently remembered Lord Krishna and sought his blessings within his heart. With focus and determination, he aimed carefully at the reflection of the fish in the water. He closed his eyes for a moment, took a deep breath, and tuned out all distractions around him.

As he opened his eyes, Arjuna let the arrow fly with precision. It soared through the air, striking the fish in the eye. The crowd erupted in cheers. The king and everyone present were astonished. Arjuna had succeeded whereas many others had failed.

Draupadi, impressed by Arjuna's skill and focus, was pleased. King Drupada welcomed him warmly and declared Arjuna the winner.

However, Draupadi was not just a prize; she was a strong-willed individual who would play a crucial role in the lives of the Pandavas. As Arjuna returned home with Draupadi by his side, his brothers erupted in joyous celebration, knowing that this victory marked the beginning of a powerful alliance. It would eventually shape their fates in the difficulties that would come.

Determination involves overcoming our temptations and distractions. Just as Arjuna and Hanuman demonstrated unwavering focus on their missions, we too can harness this same intensity to pursue our goals and achieve true success.

Now, let's explore practical techniques for improving focus, including mastering the art of studying, managing social media distractions, and implementing mindfulness practices. These strategies will equip you with the tools needed to enhance concentration and overcome obstacles in your path.

Takeaways from the Tale

- Seeking higher guidance can enhance one's confidence and clarity.
- Trusting a higher power can empower you to face challenges.
- Having a trusted mentor or friend can significantly influence success.
- Practising properly with focus can make us really skilled.

TRY THIS OUT!

Think of a time when you faced a challenge. How did you stay focused? Share your experience with a friend!

From DISTRACTION to CONCENTRATION

SECTION 2

In today's fast-paced world, distractions are everywhere—especially with the constant buzz of technology. Staying focused has become one of the most sought-after skills, yet it often feels out of our reach. So how can we train our minds to overcome distractions and cultivate unwavering concentration?

This section is your guide to calming the restless mind and directing its energy towards meaningful goals.

By understanding the value of consistent practice and detachment, regulating your senses, developing a higher taste, and sharpening your intelligence, you'll gain practical tools to master your focus. You'll find techniques for focused study, the art of mindfulness, and the profound influence of choosing the right role models.

This journey will inspire you to embrace a life filled with clarity, purpose, and fulfilment.

Ready to unlock the secrets of true concentration? Let's begin!

1 Bring the Mind Back

The Mind Is Like a Kid

Madhav approached his grandfather who was sitting peacefully on a bench in the park. The lines of worry were evident on Madhav's face. Sensing his distress, Grandfather inquired, 'Madhav, what's troubling you? You look upset.'

Madhav replied, 'Grandpa, my results came out and my score is quite poor. Some of my friends did very well. The exam was quite easy, but still, I didn't get a good score.'

Grandpa asked, 'Don't be so disappointed. You can work hard and improve your scores in the next term.' Grandpa's reply was very encouraging.

Madhav added, 'The problem is that I lack concentration. I can't focus on one thing at a time. My mind pulls me in different directions, and often, I give in to the mind's distractions. Can you please tell me how do I become more attentive?'

Grandpa thought for a while and said, 'Look at them.' He pointed out a mother with a young baby, hardly a year old, sitting on a bench in front of them.

Madhav observed them for a few minutes.

'Did you notice, Madhav, how the mom is looking out for the baby? When the baby touched the toy, the mom smiled and let it happen. But when the baby tried to put the mom's pen in his mouth, she took it away gently. When the baby was about to be tempted by something dangerous, the mom brought him back to her lap. And when the baby cried, the mom comforted him and kept him in her lap.'

Madhav said, 'Yes, I saw all of that.'

Grandpa continued, 'Think of our minds like lively, curious kids. They don't naturally know what's right or wrong, good or bad. Our minds are always eager to explore everything around them. That's where our intelligence comes in, just like a mom guiding her child. Keep an eye on your

Takeaways from the Tale

- Don't be discouraged by failures, but try to learn from them and improve yourself.
- Overcoming lack of concentration requires effort and practice.
- By carefully observing things around us, we can learn a lot of life lessons.
- Success involves consistently bringing the mind back and redirecting it towards productivity.

mind's activities, like a watchful mom. Practise bringing your thoughts back and staying focused on your tasks. Let your intelligence guide your mind away from distractions and toward productive and beneficial things.'

Madhav got his lesson from his wise grandpa and tried to apply it.

Lord Krishna's Attentiveness Formula

In this world, it is not possible to remain undistracted. But a wise person is one who consciously brings back their mind whenever it gets distracted. This concept finds resonance in the teachings of the Bhagavad Gita.

yato yato niścalati
manaś cañcalam asthiram
tatas tato niyamyaitad
ātmany eva vaśaṁ nayet

'From wherever the restless mind wanders, one must withdraw it and bring it back under one's control.'

'The attempt to bring the distracted mind back is called attentiveness.'

Bhagavad Gita (6.26)

We've all witnessed how playful children might run away from their parents and wander around. The anxious parents have to chase after them to prevent accidents or mishaps. Similarly, our minds can take us to different places. Sometimes, the mind can be stubborn and do things we wish it wouldn't.

But that doesn't mean we should hate our minds. We need to calm it and bring it under our direction like parents do with their children. If we allow our minds to indulge in thoughts, desires, and feelings that are harmful or counterproductive, we risk causing trouble to ourselves and others.

Getting distracted is natural, but remaining distracted is harmful!

If we can regulate the mind's distractions, it acts like our friend, but if we leave it uncontrolled, it becomes our worst enemy. And that's exactly what Lord Krishna tells us about the mind:

uddhared ātmanātmānaṁ nātmānam avasādayet
ātmaiva hy ātmano bandhur ātmaiva ripur ātmanaḥ
bandhur ātmātmanas tasya yenātmaivātmanā jitaḥ
anātmanas tu śatrutve vartetātmaiva śatru-vat

'Elevate yourself by the power of your mind, and not degrade yourself. The mind can work both like a friend and an enemy. For those who regulate the mind, it is their best friend. For those who have failed to do so, the mind works like the worst enemy.'

(Bhagavad Gita 6.5-6)

You might be thinking, 'It's easier said than done! Is pulling the mind back always possible?' This is a common thought, and even the mighty warrior Arjuna expressed such doubts. How did Lord Krishna address them? Read the next chapter to find out the answer to this question!

TRY THIS OUT!

Mindful Breath Break

Set Time Aside: Choose a moment, like mid-morning or afternoon.

Breathe Mindfully: Take five minutes to sit, focus on your breath, and let thoughts come and go.

Awareness Check: Notice if your mind wanders, and gently bring it back to focus on your breath.

Refreshed Focus: Return to your tasks with a refreshed and centred mindset.

This quick mindfulness break helps maintain focus and productivity by resetting your mental state.

2 Practice and Detachment

Restrain the Restless Mind

Eleven-year-old Kirti's grandmother was reading the Bhagavad Gita very attentively. Kirti sat next to her and asked, 'Grandma, does the Gita have any interesting stories?'

'No dear, the Gita is not a storybook, it's a book of life lessons.'

'So, it's not for young people, it's only for old people, right?'

'Who did Krishna speak the Bhagavad Gita to?' Grandma asked her.

'Arjuna.'

'Correct. Now tell me, was Arjuna a retired, old man?'

'No, he was a prince,' Kirti replied.

'So you see, the Gita is meant for all age groups, not only old people.'

'But children like me have no time for life lessons! We are busy with so many things like studies, sports, and music classes.'

'I understand, but do you think Arjuna had a lot of time on his hands when he heard about the Gita?'

'No, he heard the Gita just before the Kurukshetra War.'

'Yes, you are right dear! What could be a greater emergency than a war? Basically, Lord Krishna taught several life lessons to Arjuna who was confused about performing his duty of fighting. Similarly, when our minds are faced with the same predicament, the teachings of the Gita help clear our confusion.'

An intrigued Kriti posed some more questions.

'Can the Gita help kids too? I have trouble focusing on my studies. My mind wanders, and even when I try to bring it back, it keeps drifting. What solution does Krishna offer in the Gita for my problem?'

Her grandmother explained how Arjuna expressed the same difficulty when Lord Krishna spoke to Arjuna about mind control in the Gita. Arjuna said:

cañcalaṁ hi manaḥ kṛṣṇa
pramāthi balavad dṛḍham
tasyāhaṁ nigrahaṁ manye
vāyor iva su-duṣkaram

My dear Krishna, the mind is restless, turbulent, obstinate and very strong. I think controlling the mind is more difficult than controlling the wind.

(Bhagavad Gita 6.34)

But how can Arjuna control the wind, Grandma?

'Well, being a great fighter and archer, Arjuna had the ability to use the wind-weapon, water-weapon, fire-weapon, and so on. By chanting some special mantras, he could invoke wind or fire in his arrow to destroy his opponents in the war. Thus, Arjuna found it easier to control the wind than the mind.'

'Oh, that's really interesting! But then, how did Krishna guide him, Grandma?'

'Lord Krishna acknowledged that it is difficult to control the mind. He gave Arjuna an encouraging reply with two effective tips to regulate the mind, using the following shloka.

asaṁśayaṁ mahā-bāho
mano durnigrahaṁ calam
abhyāsena tu kaunteya
vairāgyeṇa ca gṛhyate

'Lord Krishna said, "O mighty-armed Arjuna, it is undoubtedly very difficult to regulate the restless mind, but it is possible by doing two things: practice (abhyāsa) and detachment (vairagya)."'

(Bhagavad Gita 6.35)

Kirti, fascinated, eagerly learned more about these two key points from her grandma and tried to apply them in her studies.

1. Abhyāsa: Practice

Lord Krishna explained how practice and detachment help, but what does this exactly mean? Well, let's find out! As discussed before, our minds store good and bad things from what we see, hear, taste, smell, and touch. Therefore, our senses are a type of inlet through which our minds become loaded with unlimited feelings, wishes, and thoughts. They make us happy, sad, angry, or even frustrated at times.

Therefore, we need to be careful and particular about what we see, eat, hear, smell, and touch. Don't allow any harmful things to enter your mind through the senses. Keep practising *sense control*, which inevitably leads to mind control. When you don't see or interact with anything distracting, you'll naturally not get distracted by your mind!

Everything that we come in contact with is not necessarily beneficial to us. It could distract us or harm us too. Practise withdrawing your senses from objects that are not favourable for your overall well-being. Many visual and audible impressions are harmful to our health, studies, relationships, and so on. We need to be intelligent enough to detect them and stay away from them.

Lord Krishna then shared the example of a tortoise to inspire us in our practice of withdrawing our senses.

Takeaways from the Tale

- The Bhagavad Gita teaches life lessons for all age groups.
- Mind controlling may take some effort, but it's definitely doable.
- Practice and detachment help regulate the restless mind.

yadā saṁharate cāyaṁ
kūrmo 'ṅgānīva sarvaśaḥ
indriyāṇīndriyārthebhyas
tasya prajñā pratiṣṭhitā

'Just as a tortoise withdraws its limbs into the shell, one has to withdraw one's senses from the distracting and harmful sense objects. Such a person is perfectly intelligent.'
(Bhagavad Gita 2.58)

Just like a wise tortoise pulls itself inside its shell when difficulties come in front, we can practise protecting our thoughts from things that bother us. It's like learning to build a shield around our minds.

2. Vairāgya: Detachment

Lord Krishna suggests that if we learn to detach from things that bother us, we can develop a special key to control our minds. We need to slowly teach our minds not to get too attracted to things like chocolates, bubblegum, ice creams, video games, and gadgets, even if we really love them.

Our intelligence helps us know what's good and bad. And then, we need to develop detachment from the bad stuff and develop attachment to good things. But, isn't it asking a lot to always let go

of things we enjoy? Doesn't this practice sound a bit difficult? Well, it might, unless you combine it with another practice.

Curious to discover the hidden key that makes letting go (detachment) easier and helps you master your mind? Why wait? Keep reading!

TRY THIS OUT!

GITA WISDOM REFLECTION

SELECT A LESSON: Choose your favourite lesson from this book. It could be about self-discipline, overcoming challenges, or maintaining inner peace.

PERSONAL CONNECTION: Reflect on situations in your life where this lesson could be applied. Consider instances where you faced challenges or needed to make a decision.

APPLY THE LESSON: Identify one small way you can apply this lesson in your daily life. It could be a change in mindset, behaviour, or decision-making.

CONTINUOUS LEARNING: Regularly revisit and reflect on the lesson. Note any changes or improvements you observe in your life by applying the lesson.

This way you'll learn ancient wisdom and use it to practically enrich your own life.

3 External and Internal Mind Control

Out of Sight, Out of Mind!

Ajay had a throat condition called tonsils. Enlarged tonsils can make your throat feel sore, so Ajay's dad took him to the doctor.

The doctor told Ajay, 'You should avoid eating too many ice creams and sweets because they can make your throat feel even worse. Please take the medicines regularly without fail.' Ajay listened carefully and started taking the recommended medicines.

After two days, Ajay went to the school canteen with his friends for lunch. He sat down with his friends at the table and opened the lunch box that his mom had packed for him.

Now, one of Ajay's friends had ordered a delicious-looking ice cream from the canteen. It was so tempting! Ajay couldn't take his eyes off it. His mind kept urging him to go and get one ice cream for himself.

But then, Ajay's intelligence intervened and recollected his doctor's advice. He realized that if he gave in to the temptation and ate the ice cream, the tonsil pain might worsen. So, Ajay used his intelligence and self-control to resist the temptation.

It was challenging, but he managed to stay strong and not eat the ice cream. When he got back home, he shared his experience with his dad. 'Dad,' he said, 'today, I was really tempted to have ice cream at the canteen but I managed to resist it.'

Dad asked, 'Did you feel the same temptation while sitting in the classroom or going in the other parts of the school?'

Ajay replied, 'No, I didn't think about the ice cream at all after I left the canteen.'

Dad smiled and said, 'That's because, Ajay, when things are out of sight, they are out of mind. If you don't see things that tempt you, it's much easier to control your desires. Intelligence certainly controls the mind's temptations, but it is also important to keep such objects out of reach from your senses. If the ice cream is in front of you, you may still get tempted to taste it, despite the doctor's advice lurking in your mind.'

Ajay understood something very important. From that day on, he decided to have his lunch in the classroom with a few close friends and avoided the canteen to keep visual temptations away. He followed the doctor's advice, and as he recovered from his tonsils, he was back to enjoying time with all his friends at the canteen once again.

Takeaways from the Tale

- Keeping temptations out of sight helps in controlling the mind's desires.
- Resisting the mind's distractions requires intelligence and sense-control.
- Adhering to medical advice is crucial for health recovery.
- Guidance from well-wishing elders and parents helps us grow.

The Joy of 'Mind Control'

In a world filled with numerous distractions and increasing pressures, you must equip yourselves with the tools to navigate your thoughts, emotions, and behaviours effectively.

As discussed in the first section, in the hierarchy of the body's elements, the mind is positioned between intelligence and the senses. While the senses are inferior to the mind, intelligence is superior to it.

To bring the mind from distraction to concentration, and channel its thoughts and emotions effectively, you need to do two things:

1. **Regulate your senses externally**
2. **Sharpen your intelligence internally**

1. Regulating the Senses

The senses act as the entry points through which the mind receives various impressions. Therefore, we must also try to control our senses from overindulging in sense objects. By doing so, we restrict unnecessary inputs to the mind and thus, regulate the mind's distractions.

For instance, when we are walking on the street, it's not necessary to continuously look at everything around us as this would overload the mind with multiple visual impressions, leading to unnecessary thoughts and desires. The same principle applies to the other senses. This is the overall way to regulate the mind.

Thus, just like Ajay, if we can control our senses, our minds can also be controlled in the same way. Out of sight, out of mind!

2. Sharpening the Intelligence

Although keeping distractions physically out of sight is a good way to control the mind, it's not just about that. Our thoughts can distract us, too. For instance, when we're studying, we might put our phones away in another room to stay focused. However, our minds might tempt us to go look for it in between our lessons. If we keep dwelling on these thoughts, we will get distracted. Thus, it's important to control our thoughts as well. With sharp intelligence, we should dismiss unnecessary thoughts and desires that pop up in our minds.

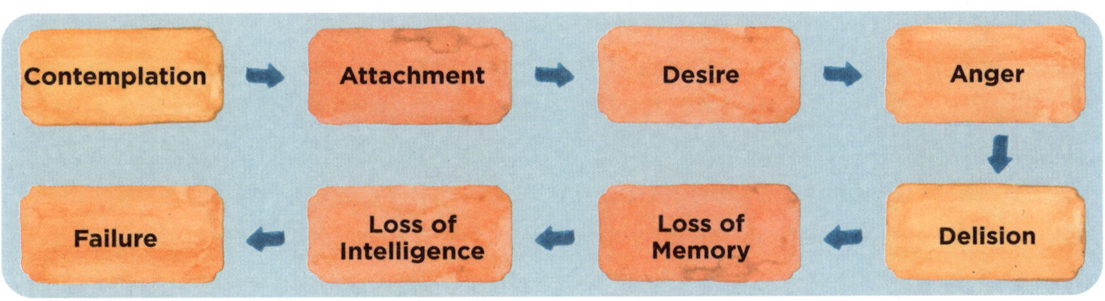

Paying heed to distracting thoughts can lead to decreased productivity and poor regulation of emotions, as Lord Krishna mentions in the following verse.

dhyāyato viṣayān puṁsaḥ
saṅgas teṣūpajāyate
saṅgāt sañjāyate kāmaḥ
kāmāt krodho 'bhijāyate
krodhād bhavati sammohaḥ
sammohāt smṛti-vibhramaḥ
smṛti-bhraṁśād buddhi-nāśo
buddhi-nāśāt praṇaśyati

'While contemplating objects, one develops an attachment for them. From such attachment, intense desire develops. When that desire is unfulfilled, anger arises. From anger, complete delusion arises. From delusion loss of memory. When memory is lost, intelligence is lost. When intelligence is lost, one becomes a failure.'

(Bhagavad Gita 2.62-63)

Mindfulness means being aware of what's happening inside your mind and in your surroundings. It can be achieved when we have sound intelligence that can analyse the thoughts and desires of the mind and regulate them.

Think of a person sorting colourful balls into different categories like red and green. In the same way, we can use our intelligence to sort out the thoughts in our minds. We should pay attention to the thoughts that are important and helpful and ignore the ones that are not. When we do this, we become smarter and avoid getting distracted.

Enhancing our intelligence is vital for mastering our mind and effectively applying the solutions of 'practice' and 'detachment' that we learnt in the previous chapter.

1. **Read Wisdom Books:** Just like we read fun storybooks and school textbooks, we also need to read books that impart practical wisdom like the Bhagavad Gita, *Panchatantra*, *Hitopadesh*, Ramayana, Mahabharat, and so on. Such books teach us important life lessons and equip us to make the right choices in life. They also refine our intelligence and help us stay strong amidst the setbacks of life. With such refined intelligence, we will be able to regulate the mind's desires and feelings. Such books help us develop emotional resilience and the art of smart work.

2. Learn from Grown-ups: We can learn from experienced well-wishers like our parents, teachers, older siblings, and other trustworthy grown-ups. As they are more experienced and intelligent than us, they can guide us on how to do the right things. Listening to elders is wonderful for inner growth. Apart from teachers who teach technical subjects, it's important to also have a spiritual guide who trains us in morality, virtues, and ideals. That equips our intelligence to deal with the mind's distractions.

By being careful about what we pay attention to, we can be more mindful of our thoughts and actions. So, remember to use your 'sorting' brain and make wise choices to stay on track and not get distracted!

Thus, by controlling the senses and enhancing our intelligence to sort out thoughts, we can take our minds from distraction to concentration.

The mind can be brought from distraction to concentration, by using enhanced intelligence to analyse its thoughts and align them with moral values.

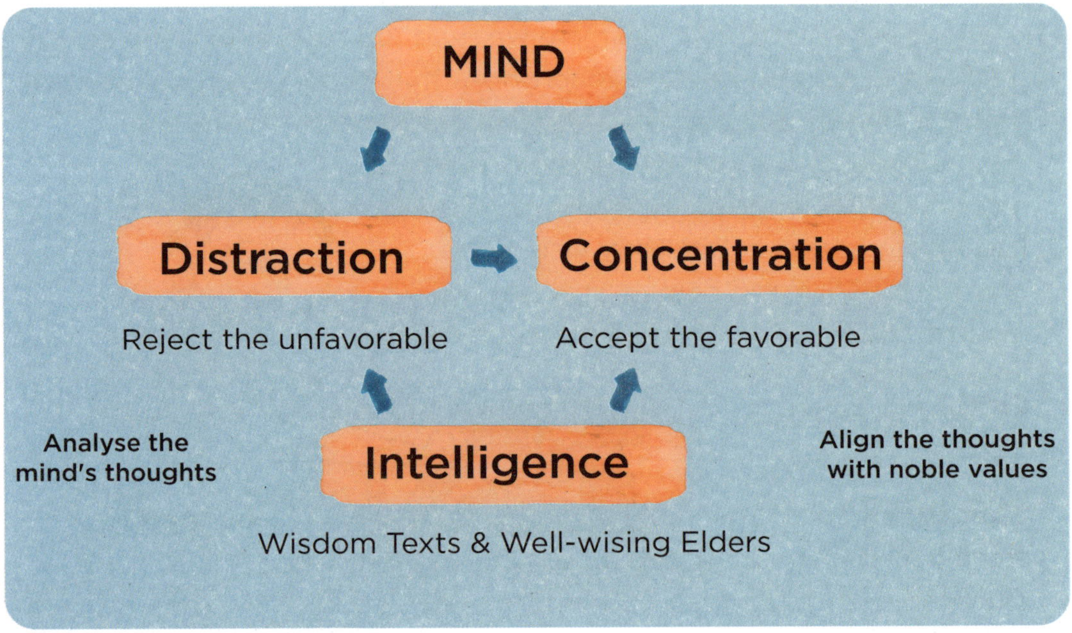

We've learned a lot of techniques for controlling the mind. Congratulations on becoming a Mind Master! Now, let's explore a few more practical tips based on this wisdom that'll make us more joyful in our lives. The next two chapters talk about the art of managing things effectively, the dangers of multitasking, and the secret behind becoming that smarty in class! So, why wait? Flip forward!

TRY THIS OUT!

Family Wisdom Circle

Gather in a Circle: Have family members sit in a circle, creating an inclusive and intimate space.

Storytelling Time: Start with an elder or parent sharing a personal story from their past. It could be a life lesson, a memorable experience, or a family tradition.

Pass the Story Torch: After each story, pass a symbolic object to the next person in the circle, giving them the opportunity to share their own story or ask questions.

Active Listening: Emphasize active listening within the circle, creating an environment where everyone feels heard and respected.

Reflect and Connect: Conclude the session with a brief discussion, allowing family members to reflect and discuss the lessons imparted from the shared stories.

This activity fosters a strong sense of connection, encourages open communication, and provides a platform for the exchange of valuable life experiences and advice within the family.

4 Is Multitasking Bad?

All at Once!

Yuvaraj was a clever kid. He was super enthusiastic all the time and was known for his extraordinary ability to do many things at a time.

One day, he came back from school a little late, and it was already time to watch his favourite cartoon show on the TV. But he had to complete his homework, too. He then decided to showcase his talent by juggling homework, watching cartoons, and eating a snack all at once. His elder sister watched him doing all this in haste, thinking that he was nothing short of a superhero.

Yuvaraj impressively managed to finish his homework. He also enjoyed his snack while watching thirty minutes of his favourite cartoon. He thought he was a great multitasker.

His sister picked up his book and added, 'Yuvaraj, I see some mistakes and curious doodles in your homework. Some snack pieces have also fallen on the table.'

Yuvaraj understood what she meant. His tummy was also hurting from eating his food so quickly. His mother, who noticed all this from afar, advised him with affection. 'Yuvaraj, if you don't chew properly and just gulp your meal, your digestive system will suffer. You already coughed twice while eating. Why don't you just eat slowly? If you just spent five more minutes finishing your snack, you could have enjoyed it properly and avoided spilling it on your table.'

Yuvaraj took in what his sister and mother said positively. He corrected his mistakes and cleaned the mess he had created.

Takeaways from the Tale

- Multitasking can lead to mistakes.
- Proper focus on one task at a time ensures better results.
- Chewing food slowly aids digestion and prevents spills, minimizing wastage.
- Learning to prioritize tasks helps avoid mishaps and enhances overall efficiency.
- Focus on quality over quantity.

Two Sides of Multitasking

Multitasking is doing more than one thing at the same time. Now, imagine you have multiple talents. You can read, draw, play, sing, dance, walk, jump, and so on. Multitasking is to do all or some of them simultaneously.

The playful and mischievous mind sometimes likes to suggest many ideas at once. When you're working on something, it might nudge you to try something else, creating a bit of a juggling act. This tendency to multitask, or do several things at the same time, can be a bit tricky.

Multitasking has two sides like a coin. On one side, it can make us more efficient and get more things done. Imagine being able to handle homework, chatting with friends, and maybe even doodling—all at once! That sounds pretty cool, right?

But here's the catch. Just like a misbehaving friend, too much multitasking can lead to problems. It might make it hard to focus on one thing, and suddenly, you find yourself overwhelmed with too many tasks. It's like trying to juggle too many balls at once—it can get tricky!

So, when we guide our minds with our smart thinking, multitasking can be like having a helpful friend. We can do different things smoothly and efficiently. But if we let our minds wander off in too many directions, it can turn into a bit of an enemy, making it hard to concentrate on anything. It's all about finding the right balance!

Now let us see the defects and benefits of multitasking.

Drawbacks of Multitasking

The use of technology, particularly smartphones and social media, has made multitasking more prevalent. However, constantly switching between tasks can lead to decreased productivity and increased errors. Multitasking can pose several challenges, impacting your emotional, and social development. Here are some potential problems associated with multitasking:

1. **Reduced focus:** Multitasking often leads to a divided focus, making it challenging to concentrate on one task fully. This can result in reduced attention to detail and lower overall task performance.
2. **Impaired learning:** When you try to multitask, such as doing homework while watching TV or using social media, it can affect your concentration and thus, your ability to learn and retain new concepts will be impaired. You may struggle to absorb information effectively or produce quality work due to divided attention.
3. **Decreased productivity:** Multitasking makes you feel that you can increase your productivity, but it often results in delaying your work. It causes slower completion times and decreased efficiency.

Juggling multiple tasks simultaneously can lead to more errors and a need for additional time to correct them.

4. **Increased stress:** Constantly switching between tasks can create stress and anxiety. The pressure to manage multiple activities simultaneously can make you feel overwhelmed and a sense of not being able to meet expectations.
5. **Quality vs. Quantity:** Multitasking can compromise the quality of work in favour of quantity. Individuals may complete more tasks, but each task may be done with less precision and attention to detail.

So, it's important that you focus on one task at a time. This helps with effective time management and concentration skills. Prioritize and manage your tasks sequentially and it will improve your overall well-being and performance.

The Art of Managing Things Effectively

After having gone through several drawbacks of multitasking, do you think multitasking is completely bad? Not really. It has its benefits when done mindfully by a capable person. Effective multitasking is a time-saver and productivity enhancer.

Now about the art of managing things effectively, here are a few tips which can help you manage various things effectively and not lose your concentration at the same time:

1. **Task type:** Multitasking can be more effective and really useful when tasks are simple, routine, or automatic. For example, talking to your brother or sister while doing simple household chores may not hinder your performance. However, keeping a 200 MB file for download in the background and working on a Word document at the same time is attempting to multitask with intricate or demanding activities and may lead to errors and reduced overall performance.
2. **Task compatibility:** Multitasking is more feasible when combining tasks that complement each other. For instance, imagine you

are drawing a beautiful landscape on a canvas sheet. While doing it, you may wish to hear pleasing instrumental music or a melodious song that helps you concentrate and draw well. This kind of multitasking improves your performance, instead of hindering it. But if you listen to a song while working on a serious mathematics problem, it affects your performance significantly.

3. **Individual abilities:** Some people find it easy to do lots of things together, while others might prefer to focus on one thing at a time. Some people can switch between tasks easily. They know how to pay close attention and have good memory, all signs of a good multitasker. Everyone is a superhero in their way with their unique set of superpowers! It's important to know our individual capacity and never compete or compare with others.
4. **Experience:** People who have a lot of experience and have been doing the same tasks for a long time can effortlessly handle multiple things at once. For instance, an expert cook can effortlessly manage to make five to six different preparations simultaneously. On the other hand, a beginner cook needs to concentrate on just one preparation at a time and slowly gain expertise.
5. **Time Management:** Efficient multitasking requires effective time management skills. When you plan your things and organize your tasks properly, you can do justice to multiple tasks. Otherwise, handling multiple tasks simultaneously can lead to stress and a sense of being overwhelmed.
6. **Context Matters:** The context in which multitasking occurs is crucial. In some professions, such as emergency response or air traffic control officer, multitasking is a necessary skill. However, in situations requiring deep focus, like studying or creative work, it may be counterproductive.

Therefore, the impact of multitasking varies based on the nature of the tasks, the individual's abilities, and the context. While multitasking can be efficient for certain activities, it's essential to recognize when focused attention is needed for optimal performance. Developing mindfulness and prioritization skills can help individuals navigate when to multitask and when to focus on one task at a time.

It's wise to do two tasks at a time when they are related.
It's not advisable to do two unrelated tasks simultaneously.
It's foolish to do two things at a time only to do justice to none.
It's terrible to work on multiple things if it is beyond your capacity.

So far, we have seen various types of distractions that affect your concentration and have gone through some effective tools that aid your concentration and efficiency. In the next chapter, let's find some super effective tools that can help you in your studies!

TRY THIS OUT

Study, play, and sleep all within twenty minutes. Now do all of these tasks, dedicating twenty minutes to each. Share your experience.

5 Cool Tools for Focused Studies

Determination for Concentration

Once upon a time, there was a wise teacher who told a young student to read the Bhagavad Gita every day. Excited to follow his guru's advice, the student found a cozy cave to sit in and read the spiritual text. A playful little mouse would come to visit the cave every day. Whenever the student would be absent, it would nibble at the Gita's pages. The student grew tired of shooing the mouse away, so he came up with a plan.

'I need a cat to take care of the mouse,' he thought.

He got a cat, and the cat did a good job keeping the mouse away. But soon, the cat started meowing loudly, demanding food. To solve this, the student had to feed the cat regularly. Then, another idea struck him.

'I need a cow to provide milk for the cat.'

So, he got a cow and found himself taking care of the new animal. With all these responsibilities, the time he spent reading the Gita became less and less.

Realizing the need for assistance, he hired a man to look after the cow. However, he soon discovered that he had to keep an eye on the man to ensure he did his job properly.

'This is getting complicated. I need to get married. Then, my wife can watch over the man who's taking care of the cow, who's feeding the milk to the cat, to keep away the mouse,' he reasoned.

After getting married, new responsibilities emerged, and the student found himself needing money. So, he started a business and acquired some land.

One day, his guru returned to check on his disciple.

'What happened? I told you to read the Gita, but I see you now have a wife, children, family, business, workers, and so much more. Have you forgotten the Gita? Tell me what happened,' the guru inquired.

The disciple responded, 'Dear teacher, to read the Gita, I had to do all this!'

Takeaways from the Tale

- Even a small mouse can distract you if you are not determined.
- Trying to save yourself from one distraction, we may end up in many more.
- Sometimes, finding a solution for one problem may land us in a web of unexpected challenges.
- Distractions are inevitable, but if we are determined, we can remain unaffected.

Mindfulness Practices

We've explored the importance of concentration and identified some common sources of distraction, along with tools to combat them—such as bringing the mind back, practising detachment, cultivating higher taste, sharpening intelligence by reading books and learning from teachers, controlling the senses, and so on.

Now, in this chapter, let's delve into additional tools and impactful practices aimed at enhancing the mind's concentration and fostering mindfulness, especially in our studies.

1. 'Select Your Space': A distraction-free Ambience

Our study space impacts how we study. A clean and silent place helps us focus and better absorb what we read. This can be our room, library, courtyard, garden, etc. Basically, we need to select a comfortable place where we won't get distracted.

If you had a choice between studying in a noisy playground and studying in a quiet garden, which place do you think would provide better use of your time? The latter! This is why it's important to create a favourable ambience that can help us do more, without distractions, in probably less time.

How to do it? Choose a quiet corner or a desk with all your study supplies. Make it a rule that this space is only for studying. It would be like having your very own superhero hideout!

Consistently sitting in the same place at the same time also benefits your concentration. Your mind automatically enters into study mode. If we change our place and time of study every now and then, the mind endeavours to adjust to the new surroundings.

A distraction-free ambience aids in attention and absorption and enables us to take full advantage of the allocated time.

2. The Art of Note-making

Writing is an effective and integral part of your study. You need to write two things as a part of it: (1) your goals, and (2) your notes.

Goal-setting Journal: This tool helps you set and achieve study goals, turning your tasks into exciting missions. Before you start studying, jot down what you want to achieve in a special goal-setting journal. When you complete a goal, celebrate your success in the journal.

Taking notes while studying helps you retain what you read.

You may read a book, but how much of it can you remember, and for how long? While reading a book or hearing a discourse, noting down the striking points will help us refer, revise, and recollect. Before making notes, it is vital that we design a study plan.

Even in big managerial meetings, the secretary keeps noting down the minutes of the meeting (MOM) for the future reference of all the members. An effectively prepared MOM serves as a big time-saver. So, why not make such notes while studying, to make the study more systematic, fruitful, and most importantly, to hold on to the concepts for a long time!

From your textbook, you may jot down some key statements, as they are, or paraphrase them in your own words. You may even make some flowcharts, mind maps, or sketches as per your preference. Here are a few pointers on the advantages of making notes, including some tips and tricks on note-making:

Benefits of Note-making

1. **Improved Focus:** Actively taking notes helps you stay engaged with the material, improving attention and retention.
2. **Avoiding Sleep:** Note-taking keeps you active and engaged, reducing the tendency to doze off during reading or lectures.
3. **Better Understanding:** Writing notes forces internal processing of the subject, resulting in a deeper understanding.
4. **Recall and Revision:** Notes help you easily recall and review topics even after months or years, serving as a personalized study guide.
5. **Efficient Memory:** By structuring and summarizing notes in your own words, you make it easier to recall and explain concepts later.

Methods of Note-making

1. **Condensing and Expanding:** Write only the key points or the gist of what you read. Later, you can expand on them when revising or explaining them to others.
2. **Structuring:** Break down long chapters into sections and subsections. Organizing notes this way helps retain information more effectively.
3. **Figures and Diagrams:** Use flow charts, diagrams, or pictorial representations to visually understand the material.
4. **Mind-mapping:** Create mind maps to visually organize complex topics. This helps connect ideas and make learning more manageable.
5. **Numbers and Tables:** When reading, identify lists or numbered characteristics, and jot them down in tables or numbered formats for clarity.

6. **Links:** Write down connections between different sections of the book that aren't explicitly mentioned. This makes it easier to refer back and review later.
7. **Sharing:** Writing down your personal understanding makes it easier to communicate and share knowledge with others.

3. Revision and Recollection Tools

Retaining what you have studied after having put in a lot of time and effort, requires regularly revisiting and refreshing what you've learnt. Well, if you don't, you might end up forgetting something extremely important.

Referring to our notes helps our revision. Yet the idea of revision is very broad. Firstly, let's understand two concepts in this regard: (i) Simhavalokana, and (ii) Vihangavalokana. Avalokana means to see.

1. **Simhavalokana: The Lion's Gaze**

   Simha-avalokana refers to a lion's glance or specifically the backward gaze of a lion.

   A lion in the forest, after killing his enemies, moves forward and simultaneously looks back to check if anything has been overlooked or if any of his enemies are still alive.

   The Sanskrit compound word, *simhavalokana,* is generally used in the sense of recalling the past. It's implied revision of what we have already read from a chronological and thinking perspective to identify if we've missed out on anything. In this way, we must take up the lion's gaze at scheduled intervals as we proceed to the next chapters.

2. **Vihangavalokana: The Bird's-eye View**

When a bird flies high in the sky, it can see an entire village or a locality. We can experience this while travelling on an aeroplane. From the tiny window in the aircraft, as we soar high into the sky, we see the whole city with its skyscrapers, small houses, roads, bridges, vehicles, water bodies, trees, commuter traffic, and so on.

The higher we fly, the smaller they appear. Similarly, the more we study in detail, the more we need to keep the fuller picture or the book's overview in mind. A book presents many topics, concepts, pastimes, personalities, links between sections, and so on.

After completing a chapter or a book, we need to revisit its broad message and its description, as a whole. This helps us understand and appreciate it better.

Thus, from time to time, we must revise and recollect what we have studied to prevent it from evaporating from our memories.

More specifically, we need to remember the essential and conclusive message of the book.
By integrating these focused practices into your study routine, you can fortify your concentration abilities and infuse greater awareness into your daily life.

4. Overcoming Forgetfulness

Forgetfulness refers to the inability or failure to remember things that you knew before.

Forgetfulness is a common aspect of human memory. Sometimes it's momentary, and not so serious, like when you forget where you put your toys or your backpack, and in a few moments, you recollect and find them. But sometimes, forgetfulness can be harder, like forgetting some very important things.

Forgetfulness can be influenced by a variety of factors, including age, fatigue, anxiety, insufficient sleep, lack of attention, workload, stress, messiness, or other medical reasons. Occasional forgetfulness is a normal part of life, but persistent or severe memory problems need further investigation to rule out any underlying health issues.

Although forgetfulness is natural for many people, we can find ways to help us remember better! By using simple mindfulness techniques and making a few small lifestyle changes, we can effectively recollect important things and overcome forgetfulness.

1. **Create a Routine:** Routines provide structure and help your brain know what to expect. They make it easier to remember tasks because they become part of your daily habits. For example, set a routine for after school: snack time, homework, playtime, and then dinner. This way, your brain gets used to the order of activities and you become more disciplined. *Consistency can help improve memory.*
2. **Write Things:** Writing things down reinforces information and serves as a visual reminder. For example, if your teacher

announces a special event, write it on a calendar or in a notebook so you don't forget.

3. **Repetition:** Regularly review and repeat information you want to remember. This can strengthen your memory.

4. **Stay Organized:** Keeping your belongings in specific places reduces the chances of forgetting where you put things. Designate a shelf for your favourite toys and a specific spot for your school backpack. This makes it easier to find things when you need them.
5. **Use Colours and Pictures:** Colours and visuals stimulate different parts of your brain, making information more memorable. When studying, use different highlighter colours for each subject. Draw little symbols or pictures next to the key points to make them stand out. Utilize tools like sticky notes to help you remember important information.
6. **Sleep Well:** A well-rested brain functions better, improving memory and concentration. Aim for seven to eight hours of sleep each night to ensure your brain is ready to learn and remember new things during the day. Sleep early and get up early before sunrise.
7. **Use Mnemonics:** Mnemonics are memory aids that help you recall information through associations. To remember the order of the

colours in a rainbow, use the acronym 'ROYGBIV' (Red, Orange, Yellow, Green, Blue, Indigo, Violet).

8. **Connect Information:** Relating new information to existing knowledge strengthens memory associations. When learning about historical events, relate them to stories or events you already know to create a mental connection.

TRY THIS OUT!

Before you begin studying, offer a prayer to God, asking for His guidance and blessings. You can say, 'O Lord, You reside in everyone's heart. From You comes remembrance, knowledge, and even forgetfulness. Kindly assist me in my studies. Bless me with humility and the desire to be helpful.' Start your study sessions with this simple prayer for a few days, and observe the immense difference it brings to your focus and understanding!

Now that we've explored the art of studying and becoming that cool, intelligent student, let's dive into the intriguing topic of choosing role models in life. Role models can either inspire us or distract us on our path to success. So why wait? Flip forward and let's get started!

6 Chose the Right Role Models

Is Popularity the Criteria?

Twelve-year-old Rohan loved playing with his friends at school, but one day, he noticed something strange. His friends were always talking about the famous people they followed on social media, and they seemed super excited!

One of his friends, Aryan, exclaimed, 'Did you see that challenge the influencer posted? He jumped off his roof into a pool, and it looked so cool! He got more than 50,000 likes! I'm going to try it this weekend!'

Another friend, Maya, jumped in, 'And I'm going to try that money-back challenge! The influencer said if I give him my pocket money, he'll double it and give it back in just three days. All I have to do is fill out a form! There were tons of comments from people who actually got their money doubled. It sounds so easy—no need to work for it!'

Rohan felt puzzled. Jumping off a roof? Handing over pocket money to someone promising to double it? Both ideas seemed unreasonable and risky. He started to wonder if following these popular influencers was a good idea. Could they be leading his friends into making dangerous or foolish decisions just because they were famous? Recently, Rohan had noticed some of his friends and seniors, who had just gotten smartphones, spending so much time on social media that they even secretly browsed and chatted during class!

That night at dinner, while enjoying his favourite porridge, Rohan turned to his father with a puzzled look. 'Papa,' he asked, 'some of my friends follow people online who have a lot of followers, but sometimes those influencers say or do things that don't seem nice. I've also noticed that when some of my friends start following someone famous, they

unfollow them after a while. Why do they do that?'

His father thought for a moment and smiled. 'That's a really good question, Rohan. Sometimes people follow someone because they seem cool or popular, but later realize that the person might not be the best influence. Maybe the influencer says or does things that don't match the values your friends believe in. When they see that, they unfollow them.'

Rohan furrowed his brow. 'So, people might follow someone just because they're popular, but then stop when they realize the person isn't that good?'

His father nodded. 'Exactly. So you should understand that popularity doesn't always mean someone is a good role model. It's important to look beyond how many followers someone has and pay attention to what they stand for. A good role model is someone who inspires us to be better, not just someone who's famous.'

'Think about it!' Rohan's father continued. 'Just like Lord Krishna helped Arjuna when he was confused on the battlefield, we all need good role models to guide us in life. They should help us understand things better and bring clarity to our minds. Unfortunately, many influencers today create more confusion. They promote lifestyles that aren't helpful or share silly content that just wastes our time. Some so-called role models even trick us! I've seen many kids trying to copy these influencers, hoping it will make them famous. Instead of focusing on what really matters, they get caught up in wanting followers, likes, and comments.'

Rohan nodded, thinking about his friends. 'Yeah, I've seen them spending a lot of time reading or posting comments on social media. They really look up to those influencers! Can you give me some examples of good role models?'

Dad smiled. 'Sure! The best role model of all is God! His perfect actions show us how to be our best selves. Saints and wise people are also great role models to follow. So, we should follow their footsteps and learn from them. Some famous people might seem cool, but if they lead us away from what's really important, they're not the stars we want to follow.'

Rohan's eyes sparkled with excitement. 'Thank you, Dad, for these examples! So if someone doesn't inspire me to be better or teach me good values, I don't need to follow them, right?'

'Exactly!' his father replied, ruffling Rohan's hair playfully. 'Always ask yourself: do they inspire me to be a better student, a better son, or a better person? Do they teach me good values? If not, it's time to find someone who can. It's not about following trends or joining the crowd; it's about looking for what's truly helpful!'

From that day on, Rohan became a little explorer, searching for the best role models who inspired kindness, honesty, and courage. He shared his learnings with his friends, helping them avoid distractions. Every night, he'd look up at the stars, feeling proud that he was choosing the brightest ones to guide his way!

Takeaways from the Tale

- Choose role models who inspire positive values, not just those who are popular.
- Popularity doesn't guarantee someone is a good influence.
- Don't follow the crowd or the trend; follow those who lead with truth.
- Seek guidance from trusted sources like parents, teachers, or spiritual examples.

Following and Being a Role Model

In the Gita, Lord Krishna teaches us something important:

yad yad ācarati śreṣṭhas
tat tad evetaro janaḥ
sa yat pramāṇaṁ kurute
lokas tad anuvartate

'Whatever actions a great person does, others follow. And whatever example they set, the world follows, too!'
(Bhagavad Gita 3.21)

This means people are always looking up to someone, and they either get inspired in a good way or a bad way, depending on who they follow. But for us cool kids who want to lead awesome lives, we need to make sure we get inspired by good people, not by those who do silly or harmful things.

Sometimes, the world makes a mistake by praising people who are actually doing foolish things. What really deserves attention often gets ignored, while things that aren't that important get way too much attention! So, whether we're at school, home, or scrolling through social media on our smart phones, we have to be smart about choosing who to follow.

Social media has its way of capturing our emotions and distracting us from what truly matters to us. It does have its good utility in sharing wisdom, inspiration, and joy, but it also has its darker side of plunging us into unwanted thoughts, aspirations, and addictions.

And guess what? It's not just about who we follow—we can inspire others too! You might wonder, 'Who can I inspire?' Well, we can actually inspire ourselves first! When we make good choices, we feel positive and are inspired to do more good things. But if we do something wrong, we push ourselves towards negativity. Plus, our actions might inspire our friends, younger siblings, or classmates.

So, while looking for role models to follow, remember to set a great example yourself!

TRY THIS OUT!

To help you pick good role models in life, here's a list of five historical figures. Read here what they did, explore more about them, and decide whether they were good role models or not!

Mother Teresa: A nun who dedicated her life to helping the poor and sick, showing compassion and kindness to those in need. She inspired many to care for others.
General Dyer: A man is remembered for his controversial role in the Jallianwala Bagh incident of 1919, where his order to open fire on a gathering had a profound and tragic impact, leaving a lasting mark on India's history.
APJ Abdul Kalam: APJ Abdul Kalam, known as the 'Missile Man of India', dedicated his life to science, education, and inspiring millions, championing a vision of a self-reliant and progressive India.
Adolf Hitler: A dictator responsible for World War II and the death of millions of innocent people. He spread hatred and violence instead of love and peace.
A. C. Bhaktivedanta Swami: A spiritual leader who spread the teachings of devotion to God worldwide. He inspired millions to lead a life of selflessness, kindness, and service to others.

Now, let's dive into the most exciting chapter on the smart way to use smartphones! Keep reading to discover how to control your mobile, rather than letting it control you.

Aditi's Spoiled Test

On a bright afternoon, Aditi sat at her desk, surrounded by her textbooks, ready to conquer the subjects for her big exam the next day. The clock ticked slowly, each second pulling her closer to study time. As she opened her first book, her phone buzzed with a notification. Curiosity sparkled in her eyes. 'Just one quick look,' she thought, tapping on a video that caught her attention.

As the minutes turned into hours, she lost herself in a sea of laughter, watching silly pranks, movie clips, adorable animal videos, some scary visuals, and reading unwanted comments. Before she knew it, the sun had set, casting long shadows across her room. Panic set in as she realized her precious study time had vanished. She stayed up late till midnight and managed to read and revise a few chapters.

The next day, Aditi walked into her exam room. Her stomach was in a knot of anxiety. She flipped through the pages, but her mind was blank. When she returned home, a wave of disappointment crashed over her. Tears rolled down her cheeks as she thought of all her hard work undone.

Her mom, sensing something wrong, rushed to her side. 'What happened, Aditi?' she asked, wrapping her arms around her daughter.

'I did poorly in my exam! I spent all my time on my phone yesterday instead of studying!' Aditi cried as she rested her face against her mom's comforting shoulder.

'Let's talk about it,' her mom said gently, guiding Aditi to sit on her bed. 'You know, phones can be like a knife.'

'A knife?' Aditi asked, her brows furrowing in confusion.

'Yes,' her mom explained. 'A surgeon uses a knife to save lives, while a thief uses it to harm others. It all depends on how you use it. Unfortunately, many kids misuse their phones nowadays. We need to be smart about using them! Some dangers can trip you up, but if you follow a few tips, you'll be like a super kid!'

'I'm all ears! Tell me more,' Aditi replied eagerly.

'First, never share personal details online. For example, many kids post their home addresses or school locations, which can attract the wrong kind of attention. It's like leaving your front door wide open!' her mom warned, her expression serious.

'Yikes! I didn't think of that,' Aditi said, her eyes widening. 'So, even if something seems cheap or cool, I should never reveal personal information.'

'Exactly! There was this one girl who posted her vacation plans, and while she was away, her home was burgled. It was a huge wake-up call.'

'Oh, that's terrifying!' Aditi gasped. 'I'll be super careful now.'

Her mom smiled. 'Good girl! And don't forget about another big issue: bullying on social media. There was a boy who posted a video of himself singing. Instead of receiving encouragement, he got flooded with mean comments that really hurt him. He became disheartened and lost all confidence. Social media can create so much pressure, so it's important to be kind online, just like in real life. If you ever see bullying or experience it, make sure you tell someone you trust.'

Aditi nodded, absorbing her mother's wisdom. 'What else, Mom?'

'Another concern is viewing inappropriate content. Some videos can be violent or explicit, and some videos create unrealistic ideas about relationships. This can leave you feeling confused, guilty, or anxious,' she explained. 'It's like watching a fairy tale and expecting real life to be just as magical!'

'Yes, that's true!' Aditi said, thinking about how easy it was to stumble across those kinds of videos.

Her mom leaned closer, 'So whenever you come across such scenes, learn to be cautious. The best way to handle this is to use your phone in open spaces, never alone in your room. You might think you're smart enough to avoid distractions, but Aditi, the senses and mind are powerful. They can pull you away from your studies like a strong wind tossing a boat in a stormy sea. They suck you into wasting your precious time.'

'Got it, Mom. This is really important. But I want to do better. What can I do?' Aditi said earnestly.

'Understanding the negative consequences is a great start! You can ask me for help, and using website blockers can limit access to distracting content. Focus on physical activities that are fun and productive, like painting, playing sports, or reading,' her mom suggested, her eyes shining with encouragement.

'I love painting! I'll do that more! Practising hobbies is a good idea,' Aditi exclaimed, her enthusiasm bubbling over.

'Also, it's vital to talk to someone you trust when you're feeling overwhelmed. Whether it's a friend, teacher, or me, communication helps. And practising mindfulness or meditation can strengthen your self-control,' her mom said affectionately.

'One good tip to avoid distractions from social media is to remove it from your phone and only use it on your laptop. This way, when you feel like wasting time, your mind will be too lazy to get up and switch on the laptop. Thus, you'll win the battle even before it starts! And remember, always limit your time. If you keep these three principles in mind—limit your usage, use your phone in common areas, and only access social media on your laptop—you'll be successful,' her mom advised.

'Thanks, Mom! I promise to use my phone wisely. I want to be happier and more focused!' Aditi said, feeling empowered.

'Remember, Aditi,' her mom said, 'what seems difficult now will lead to a peaceful and joyful future. Stay safe and always prioritize what truly matters.'

Takeaways from the Tale

- Use technology wisely; it's a tool, not a trap.
- Never share personal information online; safety always comes first.
- Balance online activities with hobbies and productive interests.
- Limit phone usage, use it in common areas, and access social media on your laptop to stay focused.

Aditi hugged her mom tightly, grateful for the valuable lessons. She felt lighter and more confident, knowing she had the power to make better choices.

Making Smart Choices

In the Bhagavad Gita, Lord Krishna says:

śaknotīhaiva yaḥ soḍhuṁ
prāk śarīra-vimokṣaṇāt
kāma-krodhodbhavaṁ vegaṁ
sa yuktaḥ sa sukhī naraḥ

'If you can manage your feelings, such as petty desires, temptations, and anger, and not let them control you, you will find peace and happiness, even while you are still in this world.'
(Bhagavad Gita 5.23)

Our phones are tempting objects, but we need to use them wisely. In 2024, the Australian government banned smartphone and social media usage for kids under sixteen to protect their health—not because kids don't deserve them, but because there's an age for everything. Just like driving at eighteen, we need to be mature enough to use phones responsibly.

This is great news! Without phones, we can avoid the stresses adults face and spend more time with real friends.

Let's limit phone use and enjoy life! We can play, explore hobbies like painting or sports, and focus better on our studies. Without the distractions of social media and gaming, we feel less anxious and more productive.

Being smart about smartphones leads to happier, healthier lives. Let's build real friendships and have fun without screens!

From Phone to Playground

Once in a cozy neighbourhood, there lived a boy named Tanay. He had a phone on which he could play games, watch videos, and do many more exciting things. Tanay loved his phone more than anything in the world. He would spend hours playing games and watching funny videos, giggling all day long.

One day, Tanay's friends from the neighbourhood knocked on his door. They had a bunch of different games in mind, like hide-and-seek, tag, and football. They said, 'Come out and play, Tanay! It's so much fun!'

Tanay hesitated. He loved his phone, and the games on it were fantastic. But his friends pushed him to play with them on the ground, so he finally gave in.

As Tanay came out of the virtual world of his video games and joined his friends, he discovered something amazing. Running around, laughing, and playing with them was far more fun than playing on his phone. He felt happiness and excitement in the real world, which his virtual games couldn't provide. He also experienced the joy of friendship.

From that day on, Tanay found a 'higher (better) taste' in playing with his friends. He still enjoyed his phone sometimes, but he cherished the laughter and adventures with his friends even more. In time, he realized he had made the right choice.

Takeaways from the Tale

- Cherish the joy of real-life experiences beyond virtual distractions.
- Balancing digital activities with physical play enhances overall well-being.
- Sometimes, stepping out of the virtual world reveals a 'higher taste' of joy and fulfilment.
- To maintain detachment from distractions, we need to develop a higher taste that is more fulfilling.

Uplift Yourself

In the Gita, Lord Krishna teaches us a valuable lesson about controlling our minds. He suggests that when we aim to change habits or give up things that aren't good for us, we should replace them with better alternatives.

At the end of the previous chapter, we were exploring

viṣayā vinivartante
nirāhārasya dehinaḥ
rasa-varjaṁ raso 'py asya
paraṁ dṛṣṭvā nivartate

'Though someone may restrain oneself from harmful sense objects, the taste for them remains. But one can successfully stay away from them, by experiencing a higher taste.'
(Bhagavad Gita 2.59)

how to make detachment more engaging. So, here's the key: cultivate a liking for something better. For instance, if we want to detach ourselves from unhealthy junk food, we should develop a liking for nourishing, wholesome meals. There can be some occasional treats, like special birthday feasts, and so on, but we need to balance them with simple food to avoid future health issues.

Emphasizing the significance of developing a higher taste, Lord Krishna says:

If the parent just takes away the TV remote from a child who is glued to the screen for hours, the innocent child cries. But if the parent gently replaces the remote with an educational toy, the child smiles. So, we need to find better replacements for bad addictions and habits.

Just saying 'no' to bad things is not sufficient; you need to say 'yes' to good things.

For Tanay, playing games all day on the phone was bad, but by developing a better taste for playing with his friends, he could give up playing on the phone. It's not always easy to let go of the things we enjoy, but by finding something even more wonderful and meaningful, we can gradually leave behind less useful activities.

This concept is like a secret key to controlling our minds. It encourages us to focus on more positive and fulfilling activities, leading us on a journey towards happiness and wisdom.

'In the company of good people, we develop higher tastes and habits. And in the company of bad people, we develop poor tastes and habits. So be wise in choosing who you make friends with.'

Keen to discover more innovative techniques for lifting the veil of negativity from the mind and turning it into a trusted companion? Keep going to uncover exciting methods for mastering mind control!

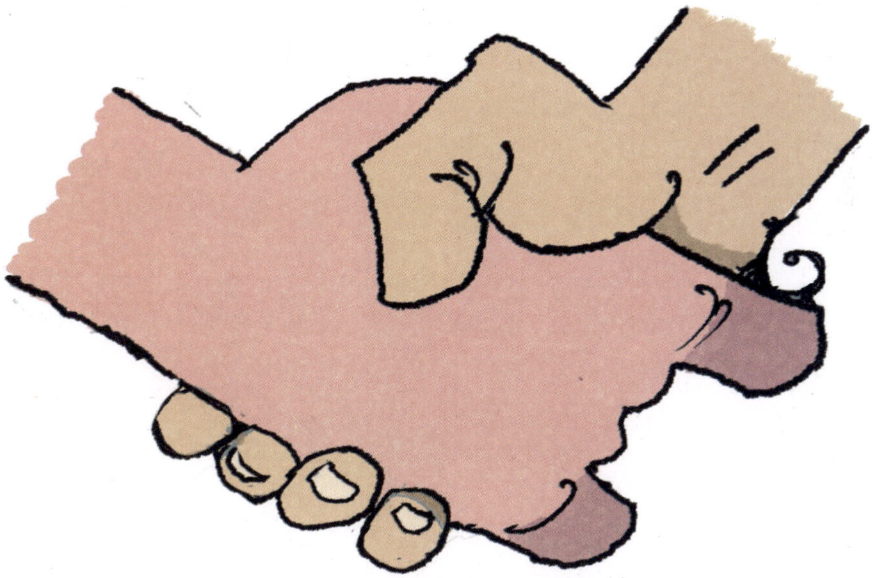

TRY THIS OUT!

Reconnect and Recharge

Engage in a 'Tech-free Day' where you intentionally disconnect from virtual distractions. Spend the day exploring the joy of real-life experiences.

Consider activities like going for a nature walk, having face-to-face conversations with friends or family, reading a physical book, or trying a hands-on hobby like painting or gardening. Avoid sedentary lifestyles. Embrace the simplicity of the offline world and savour the richness of genuine, in-the-moment experiences.

8 The Ultimate Focus Formula

Taming the Dog

One sunny afternoon, little Riya visited her grandmother. She had been feeling overwhelmed and distracted lately and wanted to find a way to calm her restless mind.

'Granny,' Riya said, 'I'm constantly disturbed by my thoughts. I tried a few techniques to stay focused. They worked to some extent, but I want a more effective way. Can you please help?'

Her grandmother smiled warmly and replied, 'Of course, my dear! Let me tell you the story of a boy named Acyuta.'

Riya settled down, eager to listen as Granny began.

Acyuta lived in a small village. One day, while walking past the homes of his friends, a fierce dog suddenly spotted him. The dog was not on a leash and ran toward Acyuta, barking angrily. Fear gripped Acyuta's heart as the dog charged at him.

In a panic, Acyuta shouted, 'O Shyam! Save me! Please tell your dog not to bite me!' Shyam was Acyuta's friend and the dog's owner. Hearing Acyuta's cries, Shyam rushed outside and called back the dog with a firm voice, 'Come

back! Sit!' The dog immediately stopped and returned to Shyam, who calmed it down.

Acyuta sighed in relief, grateful for his friend's help. He hugged Shyam and thanked him a million times.

Granny, with a twinkle in her eye, explained, 'You see, Riya, the dog represents your mind. Just like that dog ran after Acyuta in anger, our minds can often chase us with distractions and worries. And Acyuta is like you—vulnerable and in need of support.'

Riya listened intently as her grandmother continued. 'Shyam, the boy who saved Acyuta, is like God. God is our friend. Just as Shyam was able to call back the dog and keep Acyuta safe, we need to reach out to God when our minds become chaotic. He is always there for us, ready to help.'

Riya learnt a valuable lesson. 'So, the secret to having a peaceful mind is to pray to God, just like calling out to your best friend?'

'Exactly!' Granny replied. 'When you pray, you invite calmness into your life. By building this connection, you can protect yourself from stress and find true happiness within.'

With gratitude in her heart, Riya smiled brightly and said, 'Thank you, Granny! From now on, I will pray daily. I want to control my mind and feel happy, just like you taught me!'

And so, Riya learnt that prayer was the secret tool for achieving success in her mindfulness practice. Each time she prayed, she felt lighter, empowered, and more at peace, just like a bird soaring freely in the sky. Through her prayers, she navigated through life with more clarity and confidence.

Takeaways from the Tale

- Daily prayer calms your restless mind, lightens your burdens, and brings peace, just like calming a wild dog.
- When your mind feels chaotic, reach out to God for support and peace.
- Just like a good friend, God is always there to help you stay focused.

The Success Story of Universal Creation

Did you ever wonder how the entire universe came into existence? The story of its creation is truly fascinating. It all began with Lord Vishnu, who rests on a vast cosmic ocean, reclining on the divine serpent, Adishesha. From his navel sprouted a magnificent lotus, lighting up everything within the universe.

Within this gigantic lotus appeared Lord Brahma, the first living being, who had four heads. Finding himself alone and curious about his origin, Brahma tried to trace the root of the lotus. He entered its stem but couldn't discover the source. After an unsuccessful search, Brahma returned to the top of the lotus. Inspired by Lord Vishnu from within his heart, Brahma meditated on God for thousands of years.

As a result of his focused meditation, Brahma was finally able to see the splendorous form of Lord Vishnu, adorned with divine ornaments and resting on the serpent.

Offering prayers to Lord Vishnu, Brahma sought divine guidance. He prayed, 'O Lord, please grant me the intelligence to fulfil my task of creation. Protect me from pride and help me stay focused on my duty. Bless me with Your guidance.'

Lord Vishnu, pleased with Brahma's humility, assured him, 'Do not worry. I shall guide you. By meditating on me, you will gain all the knowledge needed for creation. I am always ready to fulfil the prayers of those who seek me like you.'

After receiving Lord Vishnu's blessings, Brahma meditated for another hundred celestial years, gaining profound spiritual knowledge. Empowered by this wisdom, Brahma began the task of creation, shaping countless planets and preparing them for the living beings destined to inhabit them.

Takeaways from the Tale

- Focus brings success.
- Determination conquers challenges.
- Praying regularly fills us with peace and joy—true mindfulness!

The Power of Prayers

In the Gita, Lord Krishna says,

mac-cittā mad-gata-prāṇā
bodhayantaḥ parasparam
kathayantaś ca māṁ nityaṁ
tuṣyanti ca ramanti ca

Wise people always keep their thoughts in Me and discuss about Me and thus, experience immense happiness, peace, and satisfaction.

(Bhagavad Gita 10.9)

This shloka means that when we stay close to God, we don't have to worry about little things that bother us. It's like having a secret superpower! Praying is sending a message to God, asking for peace, strength, and happiness.

In a world that's sometimes scary or confusing, prayer works like a magical shield that protects us from feeling stressed or upset. When we pray, it's easier to stay calm and focused, even if distractions come flying our way.

As we saw in these stories, praying and staying connected to God is like having a superpower for mindfulness and remaining focused. It helps us stay strong and happy—just like a superhero! So, are you ready to be the cool kid who uses all the techniques we've discussed in this book to stay calm and focused? Let's do this together, dear young friends!

A Daily Prayer to Reach Greater Heights

Developing mind-control is no easy job. Along with our efforts, we can benefit by praying with sincerity. When God sees our sincere endeavour and desire, He will naturally bless us and benedict us with the gift of a controlled mind and subsequently a stress-free life. In regards to offering prayers, an ancient wisdom text named *Brihadaranyaka Upanishad* teaches us the following three statements, which we can offer to the Lord as our solemn prayer.

'asato mā sadgamaya': Lead me from falsehood (evil) to the truth (good)

'tamaso mā jyotirgamaya': Lead me from darkness (ignorance) to light (knowledge)

'mṛtyormā'mṛtaṃ gamaya': Lead me from death to immortality

In this way, by praying to a higher power for blessings, we can elevate ourselves to higher levels of consciousness.

TRY THIS OUT!

A SIMPLE PRAYER

'O Lord Krishna, just as you became the charioteer of your friend Arjuna, please be the charioteer of my mind and kindly guide me in the right direction.'

Try chanting this prayer for a few days and see the magic it brings into your life!

Acknowledgements

Words fall short of expressing my gratitude to Srila Prabhupada, the founder Acharya of the International Society for Krishna Consciousness, who presented the magnum opus literature, Bhagavad Gita, with his lucid explanations. It is through the lens of his illuminating purports that I have learnt to understand the depth of the Gita.

I am forever indebted to my beloved guru, His Holiness Radhanath Swami, the founder of Govardhan Ecovillage and an international bestselling author, for enlightening me on the ideal mood of scriptural study and encouraging me with his kind blessings. I learnt profound truths of life by hearing his discourses and by observing his exemplary dealings. I express my earnest gratitude to Gauranga Prabhu and many other great spiritual teachers and friends who inspired me in various ways in my spiritual journey.

I am deeply grateful to Tanay Shah for his enthusiastic contributions and for patiently editing the manuscript. My heartfelt thanks also go to Parth Shah for his encouraging suggestions. With the honest and selfless efforts of these two young friends, this book has taken such a beautiful shape.

A special thanks to Ashley Kumar and Prerna Mathur for their meticulous editing and seamless coordination in bringing this book to life. I sincerely appreciate Charbak Dipta for his captivating illustrations, which greatly enhance the book's appeal and make its contents easily accessible to children.

Finally, I heartily thank all the wonderful children who attended my multiple online and onsite classes and courses, and gave me an understanding of their thoughts and needs through their innocent and intelligent questions. I congratulate their parents and teachers who taught them so well. It's a great pleasure to offer one more gift to them in the form of this book.

About the Author

Gauranga Darshan Das, a disciple of His Holiness Radhanath Swami, is a distinguished educator, prolific speaker, and bestselling author of over forty books. He holds a master's degree in Systems Science and Automation from the prestigious Indian Institute of Science (IISc), Bangalore, India. His outstanding contributions have earned him accolades such as the 'Visionary Leader: Spirituality' Award from Brand Vision Inc. and the Spiritual Scientist Award from Andhra University.

Before embracing monkhood in 2009, Gauranga Darshan Das had a brief yet impactful corporate career spanning two years. During this time, he conducted research at renowned organizations like TCS Innovation Labs, authored over ten technical papers, and filed a provisional patent for his research.

Currently, he serves as the dean of Bhaktivedanta Vidyapitha at ISKCON Govardhan Ecovillage (GEV), where he leads both residential and online spiritual education programmes. With his ability to present timeless wisdom in a lucid and contemporary style, he connects with diverse audiences, including children, teens, professionals, and educators. His speaking and teaching engagements span India, Australia, the United States, the United Kingdom, New Zealand, Singapore, and other countries. He has addressed audiences in spiritual organizations, schools, colleges, and corporate sectors, and on prominent platforms like TEDx, ISRO, DRDO, and *Hindustan Times*. To date, he has delivered over 8,000 hours of lectures and conducted more than fifty online courses, available at www.vidyapitha.in.

As an accomplished author, Gauranga Darshan Das has written forty-three books. His works include study guides (such as the *Subodhini* series), storybooks, self-enrichment titles (*From Chaos to Calm*, *Dhruva*, *Disapproved but not Disowned*, and more), and children's literature (*Mindful Me!*, *Bhagavatam Tales*, and the *Gita Wisdom Tales* series). He also runs a monthly e-zine, *Bhagavata Pradipika*, and contributes thought-provoking articles to *Back to Godhead* magazines in India and internationally.

Gauranga Darshan Das's dedication to sharing spiritual wisdom has made him a highly respected figure in spiritual, educational, and corporate circles. Learn more about his inspiring work at **www.gaurangadarshan.com.**

More by the Author

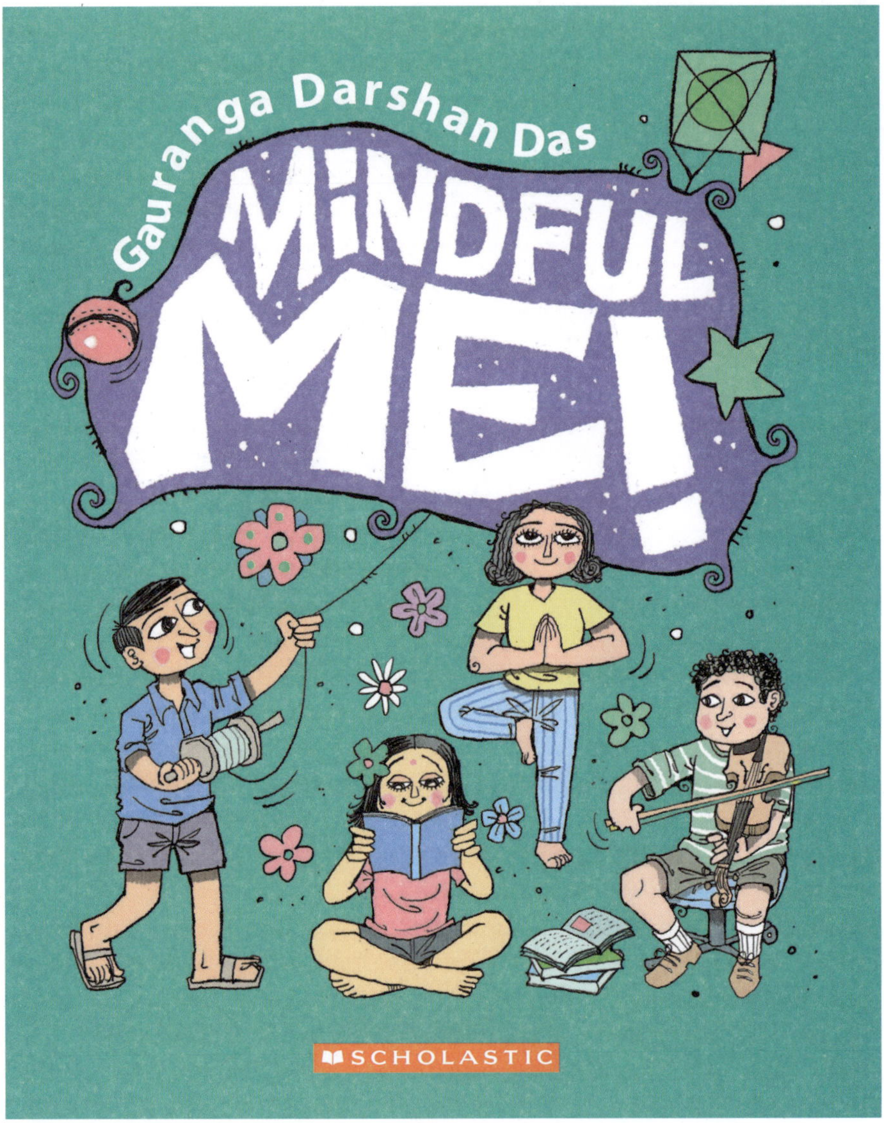